Path Of The Freelancer

An Actionable Guide To Flourishing In Freelancing

By Jason Scott Montoya

Published by Protheseos Inc.

ISBN-13: 978-1540735416
ISBN-10: 1540735419
First Printing 2017

For additional freelancing resources, please visit www.PathOfTheFreelancer.com

Contents

Dedicated To My Heavenly Father,
Who Has Made This All Possible

An Introduction By A Freelancing Friend

Freelancing. After eight years of it as a commercial photographer - I've experienced most everything one would expect from it – good and bad. I so wish I would've had a resource like this book when I started.

I didn't meet its author, Jason, until five years after that, though. We were both at a Christian men's retreat, and it didn't take me long to realize that he was possibly one of the most insightful people I had ever met. His wisdom far exceeded that of which what one would expect from somebody his age.

It wasn't long before he and I started meeting regularly and sharing many insights about life and work. I have a feeling that I benefited far more from what he had to share than he did from what I shared.

Then, one day he told me he wanted to write a book – this book – and that he would be hosting a series of monthly meetings for freelancers. During these meetings, he planned to review the eight vital achievements of a successful freelancer contained within these pages. He wanted to get our feedback at the meetings as he wrote the book and invited me to take part in them.

He didn't have to ask twice. I was all in.

Life in freelancing is an absolute obstacle course – an obstacle course that never ends once you're fully committed to it. I often tell people that it's not just something you do – it's a lifestyle you live. It can be immensely rewarding, but can also be both physically and emotionally exhausting.

What services should I offer – and not offer? How do I get new clients and make the most of those I already have? How about the financial ups and downs that will put you on an emotional rollercoaster? An emotional rollercoaster that can put you on top of the world one day – and then have your sense of self-worth in the toilet the next. How can you set up your finances to minimize the devastating lows you're sure to experience – and then - eventually - barely be affected by lulls in business. Then, there's the challenge of not letting your work consume you – robbing you of your relationship with your friends, your family, and your God.

Jason covers all of these issues in this book – and then some. After learning some tough lessons as the owner of a marketing agency - shutting it down - and then transitioning to freelancing – he has written Path Of The Freelancer from a place of humility for the benefit of others.

If you're considering freelancing, or are presently struggling with it, he's written it for you.

Keith Taylor

Keith is a professional corporate and portrait photographer based in Atlanta Georgia. To learn more about Keith and his photography business, please visit his website at www.keithtaylorphotography.com.

The Eight Vital Achievements Of A Successful Freelancer

Freelancing. It is both a rewarding and challenging experience. Unfortunately, if we launch freelancing prematurely, it can lead to a cursed existence. Exploring and committing to this path requires intentionality and rigor to ensure it is the wisest path for us to pursue.

I started writing this book with the intent to share insights, tools, processes and ideas that helped me succeed at freelancing. And then I discovered a better structure to help other freelancers flourish. It was to gamify it by building upon eight vital achievements every freelancer must sustain to excel.

While this book unveils the important achievements, it also empowers us to discover a clear vision for our freelancing. It helps us explore the potential of freelancing quickly and precisely. The challenge of this discovery acts as a test to those seriously exploring the idea. To start, let's review the eight vital achievements.

1. Fully Committed To Freelance: For some, freelancing isn't even on the radar because the focus of life is on survival. Others dream about freelancing while some abandoned it because of the bundled difficulty. It is the few who fully commit, pushing beyond these difficulties into a life of flourishing. A quick way to test our own commitment is to ask what we will do when paying projects disappear. *Will you look for a job or will you seek out the next paying client?*

2. Offerings In A Compelling Package: A strong freelancing foundation is built around knowing our financial goals, what solutions we offer and how we'll work with our customers. Once we know these details, we'll refine them in the publishing and promotion process. It's hard for people to hire us when they don't know how we can help them. *Can you concisely communicate this when prospects ask?*

3. Steady Stream Of Paying Clients: Finding the first client can feel like a difficult task. Tapping into a constant stream can feel impossible and something we can't do on our own. It is in this achievement where we must find new work consistently while also building a community of advocates to help share the burden. *When the rubber meets the road, do you know how to drum up new paying projects?*

4. Active Clients Are Maximized: The highest impact least effort activity we can do to increase income is by maximizing the paying work we do with our existing clients. Here we build agenda-free relationships, passive income streams, and ongoing client engagements towards a place where we only work with sweet spot clients. *Are you providing the most value possible to your customers?*

5. Unaffected By The Roller Coaster: Feast and famine is the common occurrence for freelancers, especially in the early years. It doesn't have to be this way. We can build a system that helps us prevent and respond to the financial and emotional ups and downs that come with freelancing. *Are you riding the roller coaster or have you made the wise decision to step off?*

6. Wise & Precise Financial Management: We can quickly go from success to failure with a few bad financial decisions. Independent freelancers need to get legit, track what matters, get paid on-time and proactively manage taxes. *Do you have the financial visibility to make wise decisions?*

7. Unified Personal and Work Lives: Our work quickly becomes a burden when it's no longer enjoyable or lacks meaning. When we're drained it affects our health, family and friends. To sustain our vocation over the long haul, we need to easily adapt, communicate with those we care about while also resting and living a healthy life. It's not easy to bring our personal and professional lives together, but it's well worth it. *Is freelancing driving you towards or away from your values and goals?*

8. We Share What We've Mastered: Others benefit from us sharing with them. In our journey we glean wisdom from lessons learned. This is valuable insight to share privately and publicly. It is the process of teaching what we've mastered that helps us fully understand what we know and why we know it. It's the final and most important step in our journey to success. *Who are you helping?*

What To Expect Moving Forward

It's a straightforward list, but the act of defining these eight achievements empowers us to quickly and clearly see where we are at in the journey, and how we move forward to the next stage.

At the beginning of writing this book, I found the eighth achievement was the one I had yet to accomplish. I've personally found it to be the most fulfilling one on the list. Teaching what we've learned helps us fill in the gaps of what we've missed or forgotten. It also equips the next generation to take what we've mastered and carry it forward into their work, and to those they teach in their future.

As we work through these eight achievements, it's important to understand our progress through them is not linear and neat. In reality, we'll likely be working through multiple achievements at once, and in some cases, we'll accomplish one as we abandon another.

Each time we succeed at a vital achievement, we add new dynamics we have to adjust for, making it difficult to sustain them all. Imagine throwing a ball in the air and catching it. With one ball it is relatively easy. As we add a second, third and fourth it gets progressively harder. As we add a fifth, sixth, seventh, and eighth, it can feel almost impossible.

To flourish as a freelancer, we'll need to learn how to master juggling all eight achievements. While it is never easy to sustain all eight at once, there are aspects of the process that become easier.

When it comes down to it, the first phase of freelancing may likely focus on survival. In survival mode, we have to pay the bills and eat. The goal beyond this state is to move to a place of flourishing where this natural stress is alleviated.

When we arrive at this place of flourishing, we'll want to have systems in place to simulate the survival pressures to prevent complacency and pride. As successful as we can become, both of these can lead to our downfall.

Two Goals For Reading This Book

With excellent communication and structure, we can make a difficult freelancing journey enjoyable, meaningful and profitable. As we explore these eight achievements together, there are two primary goals for the book to meet you where you are.

The first goal is geared towards those who are not entirely committed to freelancing. My intent is to paint the full picture of what it takes to flourish as one so you can make a well-informed decision to move forward based on insights of an experienced and active freelancer.

Freelancing at a distance can seem exciting, prosperous and fruitful, but there is much more that goes with it. Before jumping into the deep end, let's understand what this lifestyle entails.

For those already fully committed to freelancing and know the reality of what the freelancing life is like, **this book's second goal** is to equip you with ideas, tools, resources, insights, and systems to accelerate your success.

My Authority As A Freelancer

In 2014, seven years after we started Noodlehead Marketing, I made a choice to close the doors and launch into my next vocational chapter not knowing what it would entail.

Unexpectedly, I transitioned from owning a business to a full-time freelance work-life. It was in this new path where I applied many of the ideas, systems, and tools learned in the company to my freelancing efforts. I quickly discovered how these business insights uniquely supported and empowered freelancers.

With God's grace, former relationship building, and my diligence during the transition, I quickly found financial success as a freelancer. In the first nine months, from April 2014 through the end of that year, I generated over $60k. In 2015, my second year of freelancing, I produced $95k. 2016 resulted in another growth earning $115k, the most income I ever made personally in one year.

Today, I bear less responsibility, work fewer hours and generate more income than when I owned and operated the marketing agency. As a result of this success, many freelancers have asked how I've achieved these results. This questioning was the trigger to help me realize how helpful this information was, and that I needed to write it down and share it with friends, community and now you.

There is an irony in writing this book. If you ask people who knew and worked for me in 2007 that I'd be living, writing and sharing much of what is in it, they'd think you were talking about someone else. My follow-up with people was terrible. I was usually running late to meetings, and I disregarded how important it was to deal direct and bring others along.

Simply put, I've grown significantly through the fires of business ownership. What I'll share with you are things which others shared with me, and that I learned along the way. You benefit from the collection of these experiences as I contextualize them with a particular focus on freelancing.

I see our journey in life as a trip up a flight of stairs. There is a step above where we are, and someone is willing to help us up to their level. On the step below is someone who needs a hand up. One of my priorities is to humble myself enough to ask for help when I need it, and to assist those who ask for it. This book is my way of helping those who would like to or have already chosen a life of freelancing. It is my way of helping you.

How To Use This Book

What I've learned to help maximize my efforts and prevent stress is unique to my experience. Think of what I share in this book as a vision and take what you need now to move to your next landmark. Except the first, each achievement has four checkpoints to make each more easily digestible. They also act as mileposts so you can recognize progress you've made on your journey.

Keep coming back to the book when you're ready to move forward and need ideas on how to do so. Don't get caught up in how much there is to do and how much you're not able or prepared to accomplish. **Start with the lowest hanging fruit and let the book meet you where you are.** In many cases, certain aspects of this book may not be of any benefit because you've found a similar or better way, or because it does not apply to your situation. If this happens, it is ok to deviate.

What Do I Mean By The Term Freelancer?

Before we dive into the eight achievements, I find it important we pause to define what I mean by the term freelance.

The Oxford definition for *freelance* is as follows:

"Working for different companies at different times rather than being permanently employed by one company."[1]

Freelancers are ultimately responsible for themselves, and they work with multiple clients. They may operate as a 1099

---

[1] Freelance. (1989). In Oxford English dictionary online, Retrieved from http://en.oxforddictionaries.com

contractor, a sole proprietorship or a corporation but their desire is to work as an individual as opposed to building a company and team. Freelancers also cover a vast range of industries from construction to technology and marketing.

For some, freelancing may be the destination while others may want it to become a launching pad for building a business or gaining employment. While many will benefit, it is the one who is seeking to live the life as a freelancer who will profit the most from the insights in this book.

So without further ado, let's jump into our first vital achievement for our freelancing career.

Vital Achievement #1 Fully Committed To Freelance

We've all attempted to try something without fully committing to the idea. It's why many times we don't finish what we started, or why we don't start a project we spent so much time researching. We abandon our book, business, and relationships because once it gets hard, we're not committed enough to push through the adversity to the beauty on the other side.

Our goal in this first achievement is to accelerate the discovery process of freelancing so you can decide to move forward with it or move onto something else as quickly as possible. Unlike the following seven achievements, this achievement may feel impractical or lack actionable tasks.

A few years back, there was a prospective client that was interested in working with our company. We communicated how important it was to establish intent and understand why we do what we do. He proceeded to tell us he was not interested in knowing why he was building the wall, his metaphor for the project; he just wanted to build it. He'd figure out the why later.

If you're reading this book just to build the wall, you'll likely want to jump to the second achievement. If you want to understand where your commitment level lies and how to discover a deep intent that can sustain you through the most severe trials, continue reading. Remember, this is your foundation. Determine how strong you want it.

A Partnership Gone Wrong

A few years into owning Noodlehead Marketing we were working with a business consultant to help us with sales and operations. As the relationship progressed, we found that we needed more help than we could afford. As a result, our vendor suggested we set up a partnership where he'd receive an ownership stake in the business for work he provided above the paid aspects of our engagement.

It was an idea I was interested in. Unfortunately, he moved forward as if we were both committed to the partnership when I was only interested in discovering it.

In that season of my life, I struggled to deal directly and lean into conflict, especially with our consultant who was more assertive. Out of fear of upsetting the apple cart, I chose to avoid bringing up the idea in hopes it would eventually go away on its own.

Unfortunately, this created a rift in the relationship, and we began drifting apart. Eventually, we got to a point where I could no longer pay his fees and had to inform him of my decision to terminate our working relationship.

At the termination point, our intentions became clear to each other, and I was forced to address our differences in the ownership idea. I let him know he had no ownership even though he had the impression he did.

From his perspective, I reneged on our agreement and was not giving him the benefit of his stake in the business. From my point of view, he failed to discover the idea, work out the details and formalize our partnership.

It was a messy situation that ended poorly. While I reconciled with him years later, I also wanted to understand the difference in our commitment and connection better so I could navigate partnerships in the future.

As a result of this reflection and others, The Stages Of Commitment[2] chart was invented. It's a powerful tool for understanding the progress of our commitment and how we fulfill that commitment (through connection) with people and ideas. Let me explain.

The Stages Of Commitment

Everyone starts in the survivor stage. They're going about life how they always have. The survivor is initially open to

---

[2] The Stages Of Commitment Is part of The Island Story Framework - www.WhatIsTheIslandStory.com

receive ideas, and someone eventually shares with them about the notion of freelancing. Intrigued by the potential, the survivor responds by discovering it. Now a Dreamer, they spend time researching it, asking people questions, and finding other freelancers to gather their input.

Once they grasp the potential, they decide to try freelancing out, becoming a visionary. After experiencing the positive and negative realities of freelancing in their trials, their commitment level is revealed based on whether or not they continue to sustain their freelancing career or abandon it. Those who carry on as a freelancer become achievers.

In my partnership story gone wrong, I was a survivor until the vendor suggested the ownership stake idea, which moved me into the dreamer stage.

Unfortunately, the vendor was already in the dreamer stage, and he swiftly moved into the visionary stage pulling me beyond my commitment. I needed to discover what the partnership entailed and as a result, I perpetually rubber banded back to the dreamer stage while we worked together. This unpleasant tension led to a slow and painful partnership death.

For us to succeed in any partnership, we need to make sure we both understand what stage we're in and actively focus on moving forward together. While it's fine for one party to go forward in their level of commitment, they need to ensure they don't force their level of engagement on others.

When it comes to our relationship with freelancing, we need to be open to it, discover it, test it, and fully embrace the realities, both good and bad, that come with the vocation. We also want to decide whether we continue down this freelance road or choose an alternative path that will best facilitate our personal vision.

The following chart conveys the commitment we have at each stage and how we respond to that commitment.

Stage	Committed To...	Fulfill By...
Survivor	Openness	Receiving Ideas
Dreamer	The Potential	Discovering
Visionary	Intentions	Testing Intent
Achiever	The Reality	Sustaining Actions

What level of commitment do you hold for freelancing? *Circle your current stage.*

Over the next four sections, we'll dive deeper into each of the four stages of freelancing so we can better understand what they are, where we are, and what we need to do to move towards a fully committed achieving state. Let's start with the survivor stage.

The Survivor's Stage Of Freelancing

Stages	Survivor	2	3	4
Commit To	Openness	-	-	-
Fulfill By	Receiving	-	-	-

In the survivor stage, unless we're jaded or committed elsewhere, we're open to new and better ideas. In our freelancing context, we're open to new ideas for our work and generating income.

If freelancing sounds like a fun alternative to the drudgery of what you are currently doing, then it's potential has appealed to you. The desire to discover this potential is what will move us forward into the dreamer level of commitment.

So, before we explore the dreamer stage, let's figure out how we open ourselves up to receive new ideas.

First, We've Got To Open Ourselves Up To Possibilities

When we're set in our ways and unwilling to listen, we'll never be in a state of mind to consider changing our work context to pursue freelancing.

While I was running the business, I was closed off to the idea of freelancing. While certain difficult seasons caused me to consider other options momentarily, it was an unexpected highly paid job offer that forced me to seriously question my level of commitment as a business owner.

It wasn't until I fell into freelancing, as the result of ending my tenure as a business owner years later, that I was finally open to the idea. After shutting down the business, I had no idea what I was going to do next, and freelancing became an option because people were asking to work with me. It was generating income to provide for my family's needs. It made sense to embrace and explore this idea further. Since it was something I was familiar with during the years prior to launching the business, I was comfortable with the possibility.

If we are not thrown into the life of freelancing, there are exercises for opening ourselves up to the possibility. They're also helpful in narrowing the specifics of our freelancing offerings.

Imagine yourself in a room with hundreds of doors, each with a different opportunity behind it. Begin opening those doors in your mind and peer into the different possibilities that come to mind.

Starting a business.

Writing a book.

Getting married.

Parenting a child.

Traveling the world.

Launching a nonprofit.

Working for someone as an employee.

Becoming a missionary.

Working from home.

What came to mind as you read this list? What was missing? If any of these options were made available to you, would you embrace them? If freelancing were an option, would you choose it? Why? Why Not? Reflect and write down your answers in the margins of the prior section before proceeding.

This exercise illuminates what we're resistant and open to, as well as the reason why. From there, we can break down the walls preventing our willingness to explore these choices. It also allows us to push ourselves towards options we don't want to do.

After shutting down Noodlehead Marketing, I initially thought I would work for another company as an employee. It seemed like the culturally accepted and encouraged option to pursue. Unfortunately, it was not something I wanted to do and found myself resistant to it.

I thought to work for someone meant I was highly accountable to someone else. I figured it meant I had little or no control over my destiny. I thought it was too constraining over my creativity and I'd feel trapped in a place I did not want to be.

I've worked as an employee, and I've owned a business. The reality is I've felt these tensions more as a business owner than I ever did as an employee! These tensions are not symptoms of employment; they are symptoms of our character and mindset.

With the very real possibility that I could end up working for someone else as an employee, I chose to explore what changes I needed to make to become the best one.

I began imagining about how I could proactively communicate with my boss about my activities so trust grew and I had more freedom to do my work. There are ways I could work on side projects after hours to explore facets of my creativity that my work did not allow. I could manage my money in a way that I was not beholden to the company I worked for.

Simply put, I could loosen or eliminate many of the tensions I had towards employment. New possibilities were illuminated, and this exercise changed my mindset. Instead of resisting the idea, I came to embrace it.

While I did not end up retaining employment, the exercise unexpectedly made my freelancing career more productive. I've become the employee you want, but can't have.
It is reassuring to know we can be open to discovering and testing ideas before we fully commit to them. This is a benefit of defining our stages of commitment By saying yes

to receive ideas does not mean we're saying yes to anything more than this.

When companies ask me if I'm open to the idea of them hiring me as an employee, I let them know I'm open to discovering the potential. In some cases, these ideas are explored and freelance work results. In other cases, new friendships are formed. We always have the option to say no.

Second, We Need To End Our Current Situation Well

When we're in an enticing or entrenched context, it will be hard to leave it. We've got to increase the pressure and pain to help motivate ourselves to leave what we're doing to pursue something new.

After shutting down our marketing agency, I was ending a business and labor of love. We loved our company, community, the work we did, and the people we did it with. With a call to move on from our finished mission, ending our current context forced us to adapt to what came next.

Lastly, We May Need To Wait

Once we've opened ourselves and turned up the pressure, we are somewhat limited to transition based on our circumstances. In some cases, it may be wisest to wait.

I'm married with four children. There are others I'm responsible for, and I'm not able to make drastic changes in life without considering my family. If you're single and young, you'll have more flexibility to make it happen quicker. Be patient and use the forces of your circumstances to make the transition easier.

Let's now discuss the Dreamer stage.

The Dreamer's Stage Of Freelancing

Stages	Survivor	Dreamer	3	4
Commit To	Openness	Potential	-	-
Fulfill By	Receiving	Discovering	-	-

In the dreamer stage, we've committed to the potential of freelancing, and we need to spend the time to discover this potential. We'll dream and imagine the many possibilities of what this journey could mean for us in the future. Freelancing will likely seem exciting and feel entirely possible. In fact, there is little in our mind currently to convince us that freelancing is not a good idea.

We imagine the flexibility of time. We have the freedom to get up whenever we choose. We take off work whenever we want. We make more money than we could imagine as people flock to us for our services.

The more we focus on these benefits, the more we realize how great it will be and, if we're not careful, we'll quit our job the next day to start our life as a freelancer. To prevent this haste, it's important we move quickly to evaluate the idea before we're prematurely whisked away.

Our discovery may entail conversation with friends and mentors. It likely includes reading, researching, and listening to podcasts. For some of us who are more thorough, we'll be writing a report on it.

As we explore, we can discover the positive and negative aspects of our dream. There are always trade-offs and sacrifices for great ones. The better we understand these dreams beforehand, the better decisions we make.

A good way to test ourselves and learn if we are in the dreamer stage, and possibly stuck there, is to reflect on our desire to freelance. Do we only end up learning about freelancing but never actually make the leap? If this is the twelfth book you've read on freelancing, you're likely a dreamer. Thinking and wondering about freelancing and never starting means you're stuck in the dreamer stage. If this is you, make a decision to move forward or abandon the idea and move to something else.

To help push us forward into the next stage, we need compelling intentions for freelancing. When we find and anchor this, we'll be ready to test it out. The following four steps help us accelerate the discovery stage or, if we're stuck, they'll help us get unstuck.

First, We Understand Freelancing

In the first step, we ask ourselves and write down what freelancing means to us. We'll accurately reflect on our situation. We'll discover what actual and emotional roadblocks are stopping us from moving forward.

Take a moment. Write down what it means to freelance. What does your life look like as a freelancer? What does your work look like?

Second, We Anchor Our Intentions

For this step, we discover why we want to freelance and what the catalyst is for acting on this desire. Realistically, if it works out, we'll know how we'll benefit from this decision. The strongest intentions are internally driven and anchored. If we're freelancing for someone else or some external reason, it will be difficult to sustain when freelancing is hard.

Writing it down helps us to anchor our understanding and prepare for the objections which will come. With words, we also have the ability to craft and refine our idea with focus and precision.

Third, We Explore What It Means To Sustain The Life Of A Freelancer

Before we commit, we're aware of the hours, the time, and the activities expected of us to live the life of a freelancer in an ongoing capacity. It would be a tragedy to make the leap to freelancing only to abandon it because we are unwilling to do the actions it takes to maintain this type of career.

Make a list of what activities you'll need to do on a regular basis to survive and thrive as a freelancer. To help out here is a list of some actions I sustain on a regular basis.

- Respond to emails, calls and texts consistently and promptly.
- Move leads forward.
- Schedule time to work on paid client projects.
- Communicate proactively with customers.
- Manage projects and actions for myself and clients.
- Review and manage a calendar.
- Stay active on my blog, social media, and email channels.
- Follow-up with current and past clients.
- Network, connect & meet with new people.
- Manage and review finances.
- Comply with Government guidelines.
- Execute work with excellence and accountability.
- Look for new work when the pipeline is low or empty.

Fourth, Reflect and Decide On The Fate Of Freelancing For Our Life

We can't know everything so let's evaluate what we've thought and written, and make a decision. If you're waffling, take what you've come up with and go to a friend who will challenge you to move forward or stop spending time on the idea of freelancing

Our Intent To Freelance

While clarifying our intent may be a great step to take before we start, the reality is most of us jump into things without thinking it through. If you've jumped into freelancing without understanding your intent, now would be a good time to stop and reflect on it. This is where we'll learn if we ought to stay or change our path.

While this may seem like a waste of time, it is the hard discovery work done that keep us anchored when we want to panic. Let's turn to the formula for intentionality to help us get grounded in our freelancing journey.

The Formula For Intentionality

With intent, we've made a choice. But, what are the many little choices we are making as part of the larger one? The formula provides us with the insight we need to define and refine the elements that make up our intent. Here is the formula.

THE FORMULA FOR INTENTIONALITY

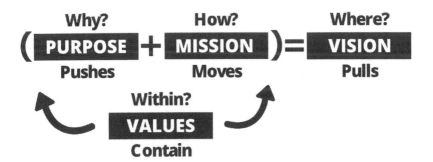

Purpose plus mission, within a set of core values, equals our vision. These ingredients from the formula give us specifics so we can follow a process to attain intent. Let's dive deeper and define each section of the equation.

Purpose is our "why". It is our most relevant and important belief. It pushes us forward.

Mission is our "how". It is how we will live out our purpose. Mission moves us along.

Our core values are the guidelines we choose to operate "within" as we live from our purpose and live out our mission. They help contain our activities and mindset.

Vision is our "where." It is where we believe we will end up, and the results arriving with us. It pulls us to the finish line when nothing else will.

Over the course of time, living out our mission from purpose within our core values results in a vision, hopefully ours.

For us to test an idea, we need a purpose. For us to move it forward, we need a mission. For us to stay on track, we need values. And finally, for us to finish, we need a compelling vision, one we are fully committed to.

Here is how this equation plays out for me personally.

My personal purpose is to embrace the life of Jesus Christ with a responsive mission of sharing this life. I operate within the guidelines of love, presence, openness, and accountability. The result of this type of living is a state of thriving together, my vision.

While succinct and clear, these personally meaningful statements are the product of years of defining and refining. While difficult, it is incredibly rewarding to dive deep inside ourselves and recognize our intentions. Once we know the ingredients, we have the power to change them and this formula helps us get there effectively.

Let's dive deeper into the formula starting with understanding purpose and then shifting from personal to freelancing intentions. Here we'll discover our purpose for pursuing this vocational track.

What's Our Purpose For Freelancing?

The reason we choose to freelance is an important one and is the foundation for which our efforts are launched from. The healthiest purpose is one which intrinsically values freelancing. If Freelancing is an outlet to avoid all other options, we are setting ourselves up for failure.

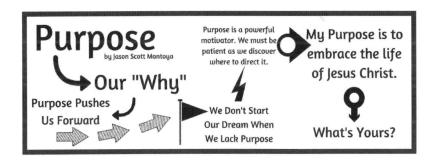

What Is Purpose?

Purpose is our why.

Like I said before, It is what we believe and it pushes us forward. Purpose provides the energy and excitement to start an idea we've discovered.

Purpose is why we get up in the morning instead of staying in bed. It is why we exist and why we live. It illuminates the meaning of our lives. When all else fails, and we have lived with purpose, we have succeeded.

Is there an idea you have thought about doing but have yet to start? A business, a book, a relationship?

The reason we don't start our project is we lack a committed purpose. We lack the why, a belief about a fundamental truth. When we find purpose in our project, it launches us forward. If we want to start, let's spend the time to discover our idea and find the purpose to help launch it.

Once we find it, let us be warned, a purpose is a powerful motivator and requires discipline to harness its full potential.

The passion from purpose can launch us forward quickly. Visionaries don't lack in purpose and they tend to launch multiple ideas and projects. Unfortunately, without considering the larger picture, visionaries tend to launch so many projects they are not able to finish any of them.

In other cases, they launch the idea and after it gets stale and the passion fades, so does the project. They abandon it and move on to the next idea, not finishing what they started.

I believe in embracing the life of Jesus Christ. The life he gave and the life he lived. This is my purpose, my why, and my core belief.

For Noodlehead Marketing, our purpose was to be an example of excellence and accountability.

Here are some other purpose statements.

- I believe in living each day as if it is my last.
- We believe communications should be intentional.
- We believe we are stewards of our resources.
- We believe in meeting people where they are.

Starting our stated purpose with an I believe statement was inspired by thought leader, Simon Sinek[3]. Having a belief statement implies our belief is based on a truth, and it allows us to ask ourselves what truth our belief is based on. It allows our beliefs to be tested.

This is purpose. Let's explore what it looks like in the context of freelancing.

What Is Our Purpose For Freelancing?

Are we choosing to freelance because we want to generate a higher income? Freelancing does not guarantee a higher income. In fact, for many, it could lead to a lower income or none at all.

---

[3] Simon Sinek, Author of Start With Why. Visit www.startwithwhy.com to learn more.

Are we choosing to freelance because we can't stand working for someone? Many of the issues we struggle with while working for someone tend to be amplified while contracting.

Are we freelancing because we're running away from particular types of problems? Running away from our problems and towards freelancing will likely lead us to those same challenges, but exaggerated.

To succeed, we need to be sure our purpose is in alignment with our freelancing. This "why" will push us to get up in the morning, push us through difficulty, and is the foundation to create the life and work we want.

What is your purpose for freelancing?

My Motivation For Freelancing

When I reflect on my reasoning for freelancing, a significant aspect of it has to do with my personal purpose and the context of my season of life.

By now, you can see my faith integrates with my work. As I share the following, you may think to skip it all together because you believe differently or don't agree. I encourage you to read through it and see how it affects my actions. If you understand the pattern, you can translate it into your set of beliefs. These beliefs are a huge factor in our effectiveness in achieving our goals.

Like I shared before, my personal purpose is to embrace the life of Jesus of Nazareth. This includes the life he lived and the life he gave. I see my work as a conduit to provide opportunities to serve and love others. This fulfills my personal purpose. This driver and foundation is important when I'm pushing through confusion and difficulty along the way.

I also have the role of a husband and father. With a lovely wife and four children to care for, I am responsible for providing for them. This includes the financial provision and time spent with them. Freelancing provides me the context to provide for my family and also have an abundance of time to give. It provides me the flexibility to get involved with our four kids, church, and local community.

To provide for my family, we had to earn an income that would allow us to fulfill our responsibilities with margin to give, spend and save. Most paid employment at this level requires more time than I'd prefer to use. Freelancing provided the potential to earn the income we needed and also do it within a reasonable amount of hours per week. It also offered the potential to limit my hours so I could work on pursuing writing, storytelling, and screenwriting.

It is possible I could accomplish all of this by working for someone or by launching a new company, but those opportunities did not unfold for me.

Simply put, my purpose for freelancing is stated as follows: To live out my personal purpose, financially provide for my family, and to give my time where It matters.

I've shared my purpose for freelancing. Let's jump to vision and see where we're going.

What Is Our Vision For Freelancing?

If we are successful in every way we measure, what would our freelancing career look like?

In answering this question, we'll find our vision for freelancing.

Without vision, we will wander aimlessly. Now, if your goal is to explore and learn new things, wandering may be a good thing!

For those of us with families, we don't quite have that luxury, so reflect on your context when working through this process. The clearer we see what we want, the more focused we become in moving towards this focal point.

So, what does our life look like both personally and professionally once we have arrived at our destination?

Before we answer, let's dive deeper into understanding vision.

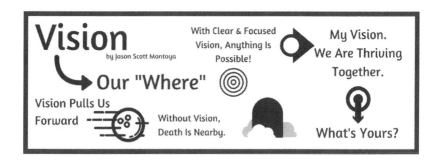

What Is Vision?

Vision is our WHERE.

It is where we believe we will find ourselves at the end of a particular journey.

Vision pulls us forward. It is the doorway of what we see at our destination. It is what we believe living out our beliefs will result in.

Vision is what pulls us forward when feelings, thoughts, and others are telling us to quit. It is in what we hope that keeps us going, and it includes those we care about.

Is there something you've quit?

A business?

A marriage?

A dream?

The reason we don't finish is we lack vision. We lack the belief that we can overcome obstacles to get to our destination.

If we want to finish, let's discover our vision. It is in our dark times and challenging obstacles we will need faith in our end goal. To sacrifice the immediate to gain the long term requires vision. Without it, we settle for short-term pleasures at the cost of our future.

Vision is a powerful force. With a focused and clear vision, we become achievers. We do whatever is necessary to get where we're going. When we face obstacles we don't wonder if we should continue, we instead think of how we'll overcome.

My personal vision is, <u>We Are Thriving Together</u>. This vision is what pulls me forward when chaos is around me. When brokenness and isolation are present, I am pulled out of my feelings of depression, doubt, and despair.

For Noodlehead Marketing, our vision was <u>Intentional Companies Reflecting Excellence</u>. We believed marketing was a reflection of our foundational beliefs. This vision pulled us to live by example and help companies discover their identity and reflect it in their marketing.

Without vision, we perish. We lose hope and without hope we have nothing to strive for or hold onto when life get's tough.

With vision, life becomes beautiful. We reap fruit we never knew possible. Through these difficulties, we discover the most meaningful achievements and rewards.

This is vision.

Let's explore how vision applies to my freelancing journey.

My Vision For Freelancing

When I think about my freelancing, I have a clear picture of my past, my present, and my future. I know what I need to do today to build or sustain my freelancing career.

We are incubated with a financial buffer from the ups and downs of work flow. There is a margin in my finances and time to adjust for unexpected success and failure.

I'm able to personally and professionally share with others. My excellence in work establishes rapport and credibility to influence my clients and community in a positive way.

When mistakes happen, I take responsibility and work through them. I show grace and mercy when the mistake is not my own. I am humble and thoughtful when the mistake is mine.

My personal vision is "We Are Thriving Together."

"We" starts with God and me, and thriving together is a healthy relational rhythm as I seek to keep a clear conscience. This desire for healthy relationships extends to my marriage, my family, and my community.

In the context of work, this would revolve around my clients and me. Is our relationship in good standing? Are we thriving together? If not, what am I doing to help move us towards this goal?

With clarity and focus on our vision, we can now easily find out when we're on or off track. We don't have to wonder if we're doing well, we know.

My intent is to model for my clients the life and work I seek out for them. If I am stressed, struggling financially, having numerous client issues, the vision I am painting by example is not one worth chasing after. My work should give my customer something worth watching, and it should be an enticing example to follow.

So, with vision in place, mission can now help us get there. Let's explore it.

Mission Is How We'll Get To Our Vision

With a healthy anchored purpose and clear vision, we now need to discover how we're going from wherever we are to where we want to arrive.

This "how" is our mission.

There are numerous ways to succeed, and we must discover what works best for us and is possible. Let's start by exploring mission.

What Is Mission?

Mission is our how.

It moves us forward. It is how we will travel from our starting point to the finish line. How we live out our purpose and arrive at our vision is another way to look at mission.

There are many ways to achieve our desired result and arrive at our destination. When we travel to another city, there are multiple vehicles and routes we can take to get there. Each route is a potential mission and each has its strengths and weaknesses.

Which way will we take to get there? Thankfully the anatomy of mission will help us answer this question.

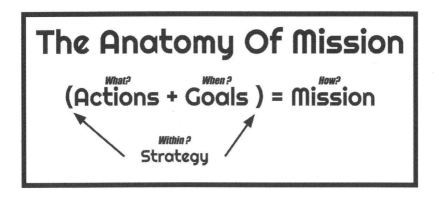

What Is The Anatomy Of Mission?

As you may notice, the anatomy of mission is similar to the formula for intentionality. Let's break it down in pieces.

Mission Contains Our Strategy. Is our strategy one of efficiency? The shortest and fastest route? Or, is it the scenic route, one where we enjoy and appreciate the journey?

Mission Contains Our Goals. When do we want to arrive at our destination? Where are the checkpoints along the way? How do we know we are on track, and when do we know we are off track?

Mission Contains Our Actions. What steps will we take to act out our strategy and meet our goals? What habits and behaviors are turning the gears of our mission machine?

My mission is to <u>Share Life</u> with others. It is propelled by my purpose and pulled by my vision.

Sharing life with others fuels my day to day. From my purpose, Jesus shares life with me, and my response is to empty myself of all he has given. The more equipped I am to give, the more I receive.

For Noodlehead Marketing, our mission was to obliterate marketing neglect. Our active hunt was to find and eliminate the marketing gaps for our clients.

Here are other mission statements.

- Spread ideas (Ted).
- Moving projects forward.
- Organize and maximize resources.
- To share, explain and illustrate discoveries.

Mission has a way of helping us to focus in on the here and now. It guides us on what we can do today to get where we want to go tomorrow.

In the business journey, I was able to explore many methods, and these pieces led to the construction of my mission for freelancing.

My Mission For Freelancing

After the first nine months of freelancing, I discovered patterns of my behavior which contributed to my quick success. The first was leading by example, and the second was solving communication problems. Let's dive into these two aspects of my mission starting with leading by example.

Leading By Example

Part of my mission was to lead by example, and this was important early on. My example was the best living case study I could offer. If I were to offer customers help in the communications arena, I needed to communicate with my network and customers actively and excellently.

If I were helping a client with their social media, having a social media presence and effective tactics was critical in reassuring the client of my abilities and experiences.

"Don't just take my word for it, go visit my blog and social network. If you like what you see, let's talk about how I can do this for you." - My Line of thinking.

If you are offering to do logo design, have a great logo. If you are offering to build websites, have the best website of them all.

Solving Communication Problems

The second part of my mission revolved around helping business leaders solve their communication problems. This fell into two categories with the first being internal communication. This meant I helped leaders bridge the communication gap between them and their team. For some, it included helping them discover and articulate their vision. For others, it was coaching them to see their leadership gaps and work together to fill them.

The second aspect of my offering revolved around external communication. This included helping my client bridge the communication gap between them and their customers.

In some cases, it meant working on a strategic level planning out marketing projects while in other cases, it meant tactical execution such as copywriting or Joomla website design.

The Three Strategies Of My Mission

With a tangible mission in place, I needed a strategy or ways I was going to bring this mission to life, and the first was doing excellent work. The second part was proactive communication, and the third strategy was explicit accountability.

Excellent Work

Whether we own a business or freelance, there is the tendency to look forward towards the next project before we are finished with the current one. The security of our next project is valuable but in many cases, can come at the cost of completing a project well. During our final year, which was our year of rest at Noodlehead Marketing, I truly learned the lessons of living in the present, focusing on the work in front of me, and finishing well.

Early in my freelancing journey, I focused on my current client's projects and finishing them with excellence. With wise stewardship, I trusted God would provide new work as I needed it. While it wasn't easy to focus on the work in front of me, it made a difference in retaining clients. It also helped me shape how I charged for my services and the way I approached certain tasks. Later in the book, I'll dive deeper into these benefits.

Proactive Communication

As we finished our marketing agency journey, It was important for me to communicate our ending. Many times when companies sell, shut down or merge, they don't communicate with their community about what is going on. For us, there was so much we learned from our journey and so many people who were a part of it. We wanted to share our story and bring them along.

Sharing acted as a launching pad for continuing to update my family, friends, and community on where I was after the company ended. I made a choice to actively communicate with my network by email, blogging, social media, phone calls and other relevant and helpful methods. My intent was to answer their questions before they ever asked.

For clients, proactive communication meant I was letting them know what I was working on, how their project was progressing and staying connected.

Many companies dislike working with freelancers because of how poor their communication can be. The client emails or calls their freelancer and does not hear back for days or weeks. I recently had a new client work with me because they could not get a hold of their former freelancer for almost an entire month. A few months after working with them, their former freelancer finally reached back out looking for more work. As you can guess, the client did not respond well.

Communicating well makes freelancers stand out significantly. I have another client who works with me for this reason alone. The work I do is good, but it was the communication that bought me a loyal customer for life.

A Quick Note On Email Communication

As a freelancer, it's important to respond to emails within a reasonable amount of time. Even when we can't or won't address the email immediately, just acknowledge you received it.

This action reassures the sender we've received the message and will respond when we're able. Many freelancers have a tendency to lack responsiveness, especially via email. By communicating well, we'll quickly set ourselves apart in a positive and memorable way.

Explicit Accountability

Part of the reason I knew these three strategies would work so well was because I was a business owner. I knew what business leaders expected because I had been on both sides of this type of working relationship.

And, this is where the accountability piece came in. I know business owners have a lot of responsibility and anything we can do to reassure them is critical.

To help illustrate the point of explicit accountability, let me share a hypothetical scenario as I place us in the shoes of a business owner or account manager working with us.

In our scenario we have an urgent issue crop up in our business. We reach out to our contractor and ask him to resolve the issue. We don't hear back, so we call him, text him and finally get a hold of him. He lets us know he'll "work on it". We agree, but become anxious because we have no idea what that means or what we can expect.

Let's play this out again with a level of explicit accountability. We reach out to our contractor with our urgent need. He responds and lets us know he will spend two hours working on the issue at 2PM this afternoon. An hour into his work, he'll email us an update with what he's found. By the end of the two hours, he'll let us know what our options are for resolving the issue.

We now know what to expect, when to expect it and we have a checkpoint to refer to in case something goes wrong. As a manager or owner, this is reassuring and valuable.

While it can be difficult, the benefits for us and our clients is well worth the slightly extra effort. People usually prefer communication to perfection.

What About Actions?

In addition to our strategy, we'll need to establish our goals and specific actions for executing these well. The following sections of this book will focus more on these details.

We've got one more pit stop on the Formula For Intentionality. To prevent us from veering off any cliffs, we need to make sure we have guardrails up.

What Guidelines (Core Values) Will We Stay Within?

When we decide to freelance, we will want to decide on our boundaries. There are two sets of guidelines we can set. The first is our personal guidelines and the second set is for our freelancing work. Not having these boundaries will mean we don't have a beacon for when we get off track with our decision making or when others are taking advantage of us.

To get started here, let's dive into what core values are and how they apply to our work.

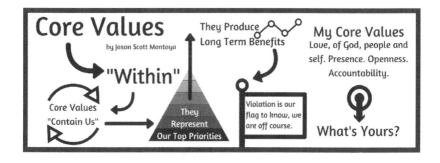

What Are Core Values?

They come from within us. They are guidelines of how we believe we, and others, ought to live. They are what we determine as most important in life. They are a set of our core beliefs founded on what we have determined to be the highest priority truths.

Core values contain us and keep us from derailing. They help hold us together. These values help us to see when we or others cross the boundaries we have set, and equip us to respond appropriately. It also allows others to hold us accountable when we cross our own lines.

Here are the core values I discovered for myself:

- Love, of God, people and self.
- Presence.
- Openness.
- Accountability.

At Noodlehead Marketing, our core values were to

- ...actively pursue <u>excellence</u>.
- ...be <u>accountable</u>.
- ...be <u>passionate</u>.
- ...<u>respect</u> & <u>serve</u> others.
- ...actively <u>change</u> to become better.
- ...always <u>share</u> & <u>listen</u> to ideas.

In many ways, core values constrain us, and in the short term can seem like roadblocks to our success. In the long run, they ensure the foundations we build in life and business will last a lifetime.

My personal core values influence many aspects of the systems and ideas I implement for my work. The same will be true for you as well.

What Are My Freelancing Guidelines?

When it comes to guidelines for my freelancing work, my personal values cover most of what matters to me. I would add the specificity that my relationship with God, my wife and kids comes above my freelancing work. This primarily affects my boundaries when it came to the amount of time I work and when I execute those hours.

It also creates a tension to give community time to those around me. This might lead to an agenda-free lunch with a friend or client to see how they are doing and talk about what is going on in their life.

Freelancing and the clients that come with it tend to creep into our lives in ways we won't expect it. It's best to decide before that happens where we'll allow it and where we'll push back. It helps to know so we can set expectations for our clients. Waiting until it happens usually makes it much more challenging.

Wow, we've certainly surveyed a lot of information as part of the dreamer stage! Hopefully, this has helped ground you as we now dive into the visionary stage.

The Visionary's Stage Of Freelancing

Stages	Survivor	Dreamer	Visionary	4
Commit To	Openness	Potential	Intentions	-
Fulfill By	Receiving	Discovering	Testing	-

In the visionary stage, we've committed to our intentions, and now it is time to test them. It is at this starting point when the emotion and passion are at a high level, and we likely feel like we can take on the entire world.

This is a good time to seek out opportunities for side work in the areas we'd be interested in freelancing. A few good places to start looking is churches and nonprofit organizations. They usually need help, and our work would go to good use.

Share your idea with friends and family and ask them to look out for opportunities for you to test out freelancing. Be willing to commit and follow through on the work you find, but know that if it's not what you want to do, finishing projects will only be temporary.

Our sample projects, volunteer gigs, and small paid jobs will give us enough taste of freelancing that we can make the decision to go deeper or pull back.

As our emotion from newly freelancing wears out, the reality of our choice becomes more apparent with the passing of each day. This weight begins to counter our excitement and our passion dwindles. Over time, we start to second guess our decision. We wonder if we ought to abandon ship going back the way we came or trying something else instead.

A good way to test if we are in the visionary stage is to see if we will continue freelancing when it gets tough. When we start and stop freelancing numerous times, this pattern of abandonment is a good sign we are a visionary.

If freelancing is one of the several ventures we're pursuing, we're likely a visionary freelancer. We have a purpose to start, but we lacked sufficient vision to pull us towards the finish line when it gets tough or boring. This doubt causes us to explore other outlets to see which may be the best. It makes it hard to say no to new opportunities.

To help move us along into the achiever stage, we need a focused vision and a reality check. This clarity of what we determine as success is the key to pulling us through the difficult times we will likely face. This vision will also determine if freelancing will help us achieve our goals. When we've embraced a vision in the context of fully experiencing reality, we move to the fourth and final achiever stage.

The Achiever's Stage Of Freelancing

Stages	Survivor	Dreamer	Visionary	Achiever
Commit To	Openness	Potential	Intentions	Reality
Fulfill By	Receiving	Discovering	Testing	Sustaining

In the fourth and final stage, we are committed to our freelancing vision and the reality that comes with it. While our purpose propelled us forward, it is our vision that will pull us to the finish line.

By this point, we've dreamed, evaluated and tested this idea. We're now fully committed to freelancing, and we're tweaking what it means and looks like for us to live the life of a freelancer.

Our emotions helped us get started, but now they become a hindrance to finishing. We have to willfully overcome every obstacle that comes our way to continue our work. When distractions pop up, we are so focused they hardly tempt us.

This is where we'll live and maintain as long as we're a freelancer. In this place of sustaining, we'll know our work and thrive from the framework we've built. Our focus shifts to small increments of improvement and fine tuning becomes the name of the game.

A good way to determine when we are in the achiever stage is our resolve to know we will finish no matter what obstacle comes our way. When we arrive at these barriers, we don't ask about whether or not to continue; we instead ask about what our options are for overcoming these obstacles.

Fully committed to a compelling freelancing vision leads to success as a freelancer. The rest of this guide will provide resources to aid the journey. Fully committed freelancers reading the remainder of this manual will accelerate and affirm what they already know.

Freelancing In Retrospect

These four stages of commitment are ones we'll pass along the course of our freelancing journey. They're not always as straightforward and clean as I've outlined, but these stages determine where we're located on the path.

In areas of life I've gone into without perspective, I've looked back and wished someone had let me know what I could have expected along the way. Knowing I'm moving forward or not is encouraging when things get tough.

In the pages before, I've set the stage for what you can expect in arriving at your decision to go all in as a freelancer. To help bring this to life, let me share how my decision-making process progressed from the beginning to end, and how I made the transition.

My Decision To Freelance

Deciding to freelance may be one we choose, or it may be one of necessity. For some of us, it may be temporary, and for others, the goal may be permanence.

After we shut down our marketing company in 2014, I didn't expect to become a full-time freelancer. On the contrary, I thought I was going to work for a company as a full-time employee.

In March 2014, a few weeks before our company's last day, a friend reached out to schedule a meeting. He stated he should have hired our marketing company a year prior but was not able to pull the trigger. He wanted to work with me before I started my next vocational venture. At the time, he needed help getting his nonprofit focused and orderly so they could move towards their vision.

I agreed to freelance with him. Soon after, others were seeking me out for contract work. Within thirty days of starting my unexpected freelance journey, I had eight projects in progress. For me, this was evidence that freelancing could be a sustainable course and one I was grateful to God for providing.

Paid Projects continued to roll in one after the next. Within several months, I was generating more income than I received as the owner of our former marketing agency. Towards the end of that year, this flow of work never stopped, and I decided to embrace the life of the freelancer and set up systems to address the different dynamics freelancing created in my work and personal life.

Several companies interested in hiring me as a full-time employee helped me anchor my commitment to freelancing at a deeper level. Ironically, instead of these businesses hiring me, they became paying clients of my freelancing services.

Each of these pivotal checkpoints created a deeper focus on my goal to succeed as a freelancer. Once I was fully committed, it took some time to figure out how to accomplish my goals but given enough time; I was able to do so for each one.

Eighteen months after I began freelancing, I had enough traction to experience and expect a level of steadiness that tends to be elusive during the initial stages of freelancing. I attribute this success to God's provision, past actions that I benefitted from, and the application of the lessons learned in the seven-year journey of owning a marketing firm.

Twenty months into freelancing, and I was sharing my stories and teaching what I mastered. I'm now fully committed to sustaining this life and teaching other freelancers.

Before we proceed to the second achievement, I'd like to share about transitioning into a freelance career. We can transition smoothly or chaotically. Since I've experienced both options, let me share some insights on how to make the process as smooth as possible.

The Freelance Transition

When I jumped into freelancing, I had people with projects pursuing me immediately. A year later, it continued. Two and half years later, I came to expect the contract work would never stop coming in. As I look back at my activity during the transition, two initiatives had a significant impact on my quick success.

1 - Connect With Community

As our marketing agency was coming to an end, I knew I needed to intentionally engage in my community. Considering the marketing business venture as a marathon, I was at the end and in need of sideline supporters to help me finish.

Three months before starting my freelancing work, I was meeting an average of twelve people per week. Spending time with people helped me figure out what I was going to do next, and it gave me the opportunity to ask others for help.

During the years beforehand, I had intentionally built a personal and professional community, and when the time came to seek help, there was a group of people available. If you've done this, you'll have a head start, but if you haven't you'll need to forge new relationships, rekindle old ones and maintain current ones. We'll dive deeper into building an emotional support system in the section for the fifth achievement.

2 - Get Active Online

The second most important activity I participated in while transitioning from business owner to freelancer was getting active online. Three months before beginning my freelancing journey, I started blogging on my website three times per week. I was writing, sharing blog posts, and asking questions. I shared these blog posts across social media channels including Facebook, Twitter, Instagram, and LinkedIn. As part of this effort, I also updated my LinkedIn and Facebook profiles. I added everything I believed would help elevate me. As a creative talent, it was important I modeled my creativity online. As a result, I created some graphics to help promote myself as well as my talents.

A good amount of the business that came my way was a direct result of this activity. We'll explore these activities further when we get to the second achievement.

Ending Well

When we think about starting something new, we can get so excited we forget about what we're leaving behind. For this reason, it's important we focus on ending well. There are many times in my life where I've abandoned or ended something poorly to start something new.

In those times, I missed out on some beautiful transitions which would have provided a better boost into the new opportunity. While it may be difficult in some situations to truly end well, it's in our best interest and the interest of others to do what we can to make this happen.

Wrapping Up Our First Achievement

Like I shared in my journey, a complete commitment to freelancing is not something we usually adopt when we start our excursion. The beauty of the process is we can choose to dive deep, ask ourselves the tough questions, and determine if we want to freelance full time going forward.

We've explored the stages of commitment to help us identify mile markers and to review actions we'll need for moving ourselves further along the spectrum. When I started freelancing, I doubted this was the road I'd go down. A year into it, I decided to put the pedal to the metal and maximize my freelancing career. Shortly after, I faced several obstacles that would challenge my commitment only to overcome each one anchoring it even further.

To recap the first achievement, we'll want to discover the answers to the following questions for both our personal life and freelancing vocation. Learning the answers is part of our journey towards becoming fully committed to freelancing.

- What is our purpose (Our why)?
- What is our vision (Our where)?
- What is our mission (Our strategy, goals, and actions?)
- What are our core values (Within what guidelines will we operate)?

No one can answer these questions or make the decision for us. All we can do for each other is provide insights, resources, and tools to help make the wisest decision. After that, it's up to each of us to decide.

Do you want to freelance?

If so, how committed are you?

How committed do you want to be?

Shifting From Strategy To Action

In the first section of this book, we dug into our personal and professional motivations. We also explored our strategic approach to freelancing.

From this point forward, we'll dive into the tactical and action-oriented aspects of freelancing. Without action, our strategy is meaningless, so the remaining portion of the book is where the rubber meets the road.

For achievements two through eight, four checkpoints are included to help you navigate fulfilling the achievement. These checkpoints will act as mile markers on the road to completion. They help reassure us we're moving forward towards our goals. To effectively empower you as a freelancer, I've put together a visual reference on the key concepts. These graphics will start each checkpoint.

Let's get at it!

Vital Achievement #2 Offerings In A Compelling Package

One of the most difficult tasks is selling our services without knowing what they are. When I first started freelancing, I remember how difficult this was. I had a great start because our company's legacy had people assume things about my capabilities. They then proceeded to ask me if I could help them with their problems. Fortunately, I was equipped to handle most requested challenges.

While I was confident in fulfilling the services, how would I charge for them? How would I service these new freelancing clients? I didn't have answers to these questions beforehand, so I had to answer them on the fly. Thankfully, I had experience building systems quickly, so I was fully equipped to structure on the fly.

But, what does a freelancer do when they don't have the experience or ability to figure it out on the fly? Where do they go?

That's where the power of the second achievement lies, and it starts with discovering how we'll compensate ourselves.

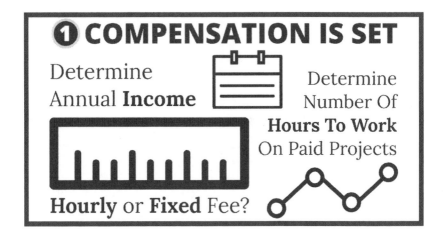

Checkpoint 1 - Compensation Is Set

With our freelancing foundations of purpose, vision, mission and core values in place, we organically shift our focus onto what income we need and desire to earn. I'll share how I got there.

How I Determined My Compensation

To determine my compensation, I started with the end in mind. Starting this way helped me get focused.

I evaluated my family's financial context by identifying our personal expenses, and the amount of money we wanted to save. In the case of unexpected expenses or scarce project work, I also added a twenty percent margin to this number. These three numbers added together made up our personal total desired income.

When we start off freelancing, we tend to forget or discount this margin only planning for the scenario where everything goes as expected. From my experience, things rarely go as planned, so it's best we prioritize the supposed unknown to minimize our stress and maximize our chances for success. When we decide to give priority early to this financial margin, we'll also find it easier to keep it important later.

In the business of freelancing, we incur expenses, pay taxes and have other unexpected costs. Let's add forty percent to our total personal desired income to determine the amount of money we'll need to generate from our freelancing work.

For us, this number calculated to $7,210 per month. Over the course of twelve months, it would result in $86,520.

Personal Subtotal	Personal Margin	Work Margin	Total Income
$3,460	$866	$2,884	$7,210

With the numbers written down, we review it and ensure they align with our goals. Another approach to calculating these figures is to decide the total income we intend to earn and determine how much we'll personally pay ourselves from that amount using the segment's percentages to break it apart.

With our financial number in place, we are now able to establish three vital goals for our freelancing business. These financial goals create beacons to determine how healthy we are financially at any given time. We'll correlate these three beacons to the colors red, yellow, and green.

Red is our baseline. This is how much we need to "survive." Survive may mean different things to different people, but for us, it is the amount of money we need to cover our bills and debts.

Our baseline goal is a total income of $5,000 per month. Any amount below this is our "**_Red Zone._**"

Our top goal is any amount over $7,210. Any amount above this number is our "**_Green Zone._**"

Our limbo goal is any amount between these two numbers. This is our "**Yellow Zone.**"

Red Zone	Yellow Zone	Green Zone
Less Than **$5,000**	Between **Red** & **Green**	More Than **$7,210**

These three goals are critical as we establish our red, yellow, green system during the section for the fifth achievement.

With our financial goals in place, it's easier to develop tangible actions to achieve them. Our next step is to decide how much time we will spend to earn this income.

How Much Time We'll Commit To Work On Client Projects

To help us determine how many hours we'll work on our client's projects, we need to decide how many hours we are willing to work on a weekly basis.

I've chosen to work thirty hours per week on paid client projects. Working forty-five hour weeks results in ten to fifteen extra hours to work on business related tasks and my personal side projects.

Freelancing as a communication specialist is not my end goal, and I've got a wife and four kids, so I'm approaching it with less intensity than you might. If you want to make a full-time career out of freelancing, you may want to increase the number of hours you work on client projects to thirty-five or forty hours per week.

One of my personal guidelines is not to work over forty-five hours per week. If working long hours becomes a pattern in my life, it's time for me to reevaluate my schedule and redraw my boundaries with my clients or myself. I'll share more about working with rhythms of rest and release during the seventh achievement.

Time And Money

With our time commitment and desired income goals set, we're now able to determine how much money we'll need to make per hour to achieve our financials goals. We'll explore later in the book how we'll charge, but even if we decide not to bill hourly, it's important we understand our hourly rate.

For my "**Green Zone**" goal, I'll need to earn $86,520 over the course of a year. At thirty hours per week and fifty-two weeks per year, this means I need to earn about fifty-five dollars per hour.

For the "**Red Zone**," I need to earn $60,000 over twelve months. Thirty-eight dollars per hour for thirty hours per week over the course of a year.

Our "**Yellow Zone**" would be any amount between thirty-eight and fifty-five dollars per hour.

At this point, we can manually adjust our numbers to align best with our objectives and possible circumstances. After reviewing, I came to the sensible conclusion I may not be able to sustain thirty hours per week, so I needed to generate more income to compensate for this. An increase of the hourly rate would allow me to work fewer hours and still achieve green.

Since I anticipate freelancing as a business consultant and marketer to be a three to five year transitional period of my life, I'd like to generate the income I need, at a lower number of hours. The ability to work twenty hours and achieve my primary goals provides me with more time to work on my other projects without sacrificing time with my wife, children, and community.

From this mindset, I set my hourly rate at seventy-five dollars per hour. Twenty-three hours per week would result in a green week. Fifteen hours or less would be a red week and any amount in between would be yellow.

Red Zone	Yellow Zone	Green Zone
15 Hours Or Less	16-22 Hours	23 or More Hours

With this structure in place, I've found my work freeing and less stressful. This padding also provides me the potential to work thirty to forty hours in a week and go far beyond green when the opportunity surfaces. I can do this to save money, pay down student loans, save up for a house or to provide extra income to take days off.

While going with a higher rate makes it harder to sell services, I'm used to selling our marketing agency rate of one hundred and fifty dollars per hour. Mentally, my price is easy compared to what I've sold in the past. For you, this may not be the case so consider your context, history and level of skills as you evaluate these numbers.

We've now completed the process to find out the income we want to generate, and the number of hours we're willing to work. With these two insights, we can know our starting hourly rate. Now, adjust it to fit your goals and know you can reevaluate it at any time. In the next section, we'll figure out how we'll align our pricing approach with our income goals.

How We'll Charge Our Clients & Shape Our Time

We'll now explore the pros and cons of how we can bill our customers. Our primary two options are to charge an hourly rate or a fixed fee.

There is no perfect way to charge clients, but there are pros and cons of each methodology. Evaluate them, your life's context, goals and select the option that fits your situation and personality best.

While owning and operating our marketing agency, I've explored and implemented a variety of compensation methods. These models manifested in employee compensation all the way to how we charged for our services. From these learned experiences, I've realized the various underlying tensions these different systems create. Let's explore these by evaluating the pros and cons of charging our clients an hourly rate.

The Pros & Cons Of Charging Hourly

Simply put, charging hourly is an easy method for freelancing. It keeps it simple and helps prevent our time from becoming monopolized by our clients. Here are the other benefits of charging hourly:

- Clients compensate us for our time, and this includes when a project grows beyond our original expectation or scope.
- We can focus on doing an excellent job without being unnecessarily hurried.
- When charging for our time, it is easier to manage it and track progress towards our goals.
- It is simpler to start and continue working with clients since the financial threshold is smaller than a larger project fee.

While there are significant benefits for charging hourly, there are also many downsides for billing this way. Here are some of the main ones.

- Clients can get unsettled and anxious about paying hourly for our services. From their perspective, they are afraid of an unknown amount of hours leading to a costly invoice.
- There is a tension for us to work more hours with our client. This pressure could result in us pushing our customers to work on projects which may not be best for them.
- Our earnings are limited to the number of hours we can work. We can't "scale" our income on services.

- Billing hourly requires the discipline to track our time while working on projects.
- We get paid less for work we are faster and better at doing.

On the flipside, we have the opportunity to charge a flat fee for services we provide. Let's review the pros and cons of charging a static fee for each project.

The Pros and Cons Of Charging By Project

Charging a flat fee can be an excellent method for our freelance work. Here are some of the primary benefits of charging this way.

- Charging a flat fee provides the potential of earning a much higher hourly rate. If we execute the project in less time, we earn more.
- This method creates a tension for maximizing efficiency. The more we get done in less time, the more profit we make on the project.
- Discussions about money are primarily had before the project and upon payments. Since money tends to be an uncomfortable topic, the less we have to address it, the better it is for many people.

While there are many benefits of billing a flat fee, there are also cons when implementing this system. Here are some of the main ones.

- This system increases the likelihood we'll cut corners as a way to maximize profit and get the project done faster.
- Projects can quickly go outside of the scope and beyond our estimations. This growth could dramatically decrease our hourly rate and in some cases, cause us to lose money on the project.
- It can be harder to sell because we are dealing with a larger amount of activities and financial implications.

When a project is planned out and has a clear scope of direction, it can be an excellent opportunity to charge a fixed fee. When we decide to charge this way, we'll want to be sure there's a mechanism in place for changing the plan and charging more for when projects go beyond what was planned.

Like I shared about margin earlier, it's always better to side with caution and overestimate what we think it will take to complete the project. When projects get off track, we have room to address it. When projects go smoothly, we increase our profits.

Which System Should I Use?

There is no perfect system, so it's a matter of which one best aligns with our vision and goals. As we understand the pros and cons of how we'll charge, we can implement a system in our work that mitigates against its weaknesses and amplifies its strengths.

If you decide to go with a fixed project fee, I highly recommend selling a fixed fee discovery process before executing the project. Without thoroughly planning the project, I've found myself discovering potential client projects without getting paid or underbidding the scope of the project leading to a loss of time and income.

How I've Decided To Bill My Clients

While I charged a flat fee for services with my first few freelancing clients, I've since shifted to charging an hourly rate for most of my work. While I think there is a place for offering fixed rate services, I've realized charging hourly is the best fit for my personal and professional goals.

I also prefer the dynamics an hourly compensation creates, and with proper systems, we can shield the clients and us from the negatives of this type of engagement. I'll share about a system I use to address this in the next checkpoint, but first, let's get practical and realistic with how we charge.

Start With Work We Can Get

When we first begin, we take the work we can get. Once we have an income goal, we need to realize that we can't always achieve it immediately. For some customers, I was able to charge seventy-five dollars per hour out of the gate while others required I discounted their rate to sixty-five dollars per hour. Receiving a client at a discounted rate was better than not making any income at all.

In one case, I did fulfillment work for a marketing agency who was reselling my services. For them, I offered a different deal charging fifty dollars per hour with the understanding their hours would be the lowest priority on my schedule. It only ended up as a handful of hours per month, so it worked well to fill in some of the dry pockets during those months.

Once we have a good amount of work history, current projects and prospects in the pipeline, we can work towards sticking to our higher rate. In fact, once we have consistency at our rate, we can transition to charging more and filtering out the type of work we don't want to do. This state is where I arrived two and half years into the journey.

Increasing Our Rates

Over time, we're positioned to increase our rates. For me, it was an increase from seventy-five to eighty dollars per hour. After several abundant months of consistent work I was unable to fulfill the number of hours clients had requested. Since I still had some clients working with me at sixty-five and seventy dollars per hour, increasing my rate up to eighty dollars per hour allowed me to transition customers or refer them to a less expensive freelancer.

The first step in my transition was to offer the increased rate to new prospects looking to work with me. The timing of my decision to increase my rates was perfect as a new client did not bat an eye at my updated hourly rate. This quick win gave me the confidence to go with the higher cost and begin shifting all of my clients.

My next task was to reach out to my customers paying a discounted rate and get them to upgrade. My client paying the sixty-five dollars per hour decided to go a different direction, so I referred him to other resources. My client paying seventy dollars per hour went up to seventy-five and committed to forty hours per month as a way to keep his rate from climbing to the eighty dollars per hour.

There were also several clients at the seventy-five dollars per hour rate but had paused for financial reasons. I decided to continue at the same rate once they resumed, giving me the chance to boost their business and demonstrate clear value before I introduced the higher cost.

It's always easier to charge a higher rate for new clients than it is to increase rates for existing ones. Ultimately, I made the decision to increase my rate and personalized the journey for each of my clients on how we'd move to it. I placed myself in their shoes and did what I thought would be best for us both. I recommend you evaluate your situation and do the same.

Before we jump into how and what services we'll offer, I'll share one other idea on how to increase our workload.

Supply & Demand: Responsive Hourly Rates

With a handful of clients, I had the opportunity to test a responsive hourly rate. The idea was to have an adjustable hourly fee based on my workload. The higher the workload, the higher the rate. The lower my workload, the lower my hourly rate. A standard supply and demand response.

Here is how it worked. When my hours for the month would run out, and I could not gain any movement on my prospects, I'd go back to my clients and offer a lower hourly fee if they committed to do a batch of hours before the month's end. Depending on how much I needed the income determined how much I lowered my price.

I thought it would be better to generate some income than none at all, plus, it would give a client a good deal. When we fully commit, we find ways to accomplish our goals, and this was one concept I was able to test lightly but could see others running with it much further.

Alright, let's jump forward to discuss the services we'll offer and how we'll work with our clients.

Checkpoint 2 - How & What We Offer Is Defined

With clarity on how much money we want to earn and how we'll charge our clients for the work we do, we now shift focus to our customers and how we can provide the most value. Let's start by exploring who we are best equipped to serve.

Who Is Our Client?

Not only is this question tough to answer, but it can also feel like defining it will limit our potential, making it harder to grow our freelancing business.

In reality, the more accurate we are with our target audience, the more focused we'll be in finding them and asking others to send referrals. A general focus will result in mediocre results. As backwards as it feels, laser focused results is what we're after.

Our target could be a role (owner or CEO), a personal profile (parent or spouse), or the type of company (home services or finance), we are best equipped to support.

Let me share about my target client to provide a tangible example.

My Target Client

My primary target is a small business owner. The business owner I prefer to work with is struggling to communicate with their team and customers. Overwhelmed and frustrated at their team's lack of progress, they're discouraged or jaded.

Their team is not getting their vision and it shows in their poor execution, and underwhelmed customers. They need a relatable individual who can quickly come into their world, sort through the chaos and get ideas and projects moving forward. They want someone who understands them, meets them where they are and teaches them a better way. They likely also don't have the time to properly hand-off and communicate what they need.

Simply put, they're drowning in chaos and want help out of their current pain. They desire someone to bring order to their chaos. It was the person we at Noodlehead Marketing were never able to find!

As you read this particular client description, you may have pictured leaders that came to mind. If I only told you I worked with businesses to help them grow, you'd likely not think of anyone and would soon forget me and my offerings. We want a target because having a target gives us something to shoot for and makes our job as a freelancer easier.

While most clients I work with don't fit this picture perfectly, they may have aspects of it that apply to them. Those are the areas where we work together.

Knowing who we work with is our first step. Now we want to paint the vision of the world we're going to create while working with our customer.

How We Discover Vision For Our Clients

Before we talk about a vision for our clients, ideally we've established one for ourselves. To empower us and our customers, alignment in our respective visions is crucial.

The best step we take towards establishing a vision for our customer starts with us jumping into their shoes, facing their thorny problem and painting the solution we would hope someone would paint for us. It's the golden rule.

Figure out who you want to help and consider what they care about, what they are fearful of and establish a vision that proactively addresses all of these issues before the client is even aware they exist. With this type of a compelling vision, the rest of what we need to succeed in our work with them will become apparent.

Skills, Experience, Personality & Strengths

When we begin evaluating how we can serve our customers, a good first step is to identify our skills and experience as well as our personality and strengths.

When I began freelancing, I had several skills I brought to the table. It ranged from leading and running a company all the way down to writing and building websites. My background was in an internet marketing agency, a technology company, the entertainment industry and the political realm.

During the halftime of the seven year Noodlehead Marketing journey, I discovered a pattern in my history. It was four threads which found their way in everything I did.

First was my ability to face and overcome problems. My mindset is focused not on whether I can solve it, but instead on my options for resolving the challenge.

The second skill was my love for storytelling. I found myself communicating complex concepts in ways others could understand and enjoy. My ability to tell stories helped bring others along, reassuring them we were moving in the desired direction. This soft skill led to several tangible outlets including my capability to write.

The third was my strength to bring people together. We moved to Atlanta in 2005, and when we went back home to visit Arizona, I had a friend who told me I was the bringer of people. I had a way of moving a network of individuals to participate in events, movements and towards a vision. I enjoyed and excelled at this feat and appreciated the many responses people had to these gatherings.

The fourth and last thread woven in my being was the skill of orchestrating people with others, resources, ideas, and technology. I understand how to equip people with what they need to succeed, and I connect them with technology and resources to help accelerate the journey towards their goals.

Once I realized these four patterns, it became freeing. It opened up the possibilities to explore many trades as long as it encapsulated these giftings. Working within these areas allows me to generate income, enjoy my work, do something meaningful and achieve results.

Personality & Strengths

To take what we've discussed deeper, I encourage learning more about your personality type and strengths. In my life's journey, I learned more about my personality profile, and it helped me better understand myself and how to work with others. It was especially useful in understanding my wife and how she sees the world.

There are two main personality profile tests we can take, and I'd encourage taking them both. The first is a Myers-Briggs or Jung test, and the second is a DISC test[4]. When you're able, I'd also recommend spending the money to take these tests with an in-depth reporting company.

In addition to personality testing, another one I found valuable was Strengths Finder 2.0[5]. It was super helpful to better understand my skills and where I could excel. I encourage you to pick up a copy of this short book which includes a code to take the test online. The better we know ourselves, the better equipped we are to help our customers.

Batch Action Management (BAM)

A few months into my freelancing journey, I set out to create an action management and communication system encouraging excellent work, accountability, proactive communication, and flexibility. Also, creating a fair system for both myself and the client was crucial to how I designed it.

With a variety of different experiences in my back pocket and the insight of a business owner, I decided to start with

---

[4] A free version of JUNG & DISC tests can be found at 123test.com. A Fun Myers-Briggs test can be found at 16personalities.com.
[5] You can learn more about Strengths Finder 2.0 at www.strengthsfinder.com

an hourly service model as the foundation for the BAM system.

Every system generates positive and negative dynamics, and an hourly system is no exception. While an hourly model gave the most flexibility to the client and fairness to the freelancer, it also generated anxiety for a customer concerned about spending more money than they are willing. As a former business owner paying contractors hourly, I know how easy it is for freelancers to rack up their time and generate a costly invoice owners were not expecting or ready to pay.

To prevent and minimize this negative dynamic I decided to inject a **CAP** on the hours so a client could commit to and know how much they would pay for services upfront. Ten hours was the realistic number with which I started. At seventy-five dollars per hour, a client was committing to seven hundred and fifty dollars per **BATCH**.

The cap element is reassuring for clients. They know they've committed to a set amount of hours. No business leader wants to blink an eye and realize their contractor logged forty hours unbeknownst to them.

I've also had situations in our past business where hired vendors completed low priority work before urgent items. In other cases, I've experienced providers completing tasks that were not important to us all.

To ensure the highest impact lowest effort tasks were completed first, I implemented two communication checkpoints during the batch's progress. These communication **CHECKPOINTS** would allow me as a freelancer to get organized and focused on the work I was doing for the client.

It would also provide the client an opportunity to prioritize my efforts and pivot when urgent issues arose. Simply put, it gives our customers a steering wheel to drive us, especially when they need us to go a different direction.

These updates allow the customer to take a pulse on what we're working on next, the hours going by as well as empowering them to redirect our efforts going forward.

The Batch Action Management (BAM) system involves high levels of communication and accountability to encourage accuracy and high performance.

For clients that have tested the waters and are comfortable working with me in this system, we now discuss working at a **PACE** they're comfortable with. Pace is the number of batches we'll complete in a designated timeframe. The pace can be the number of batches we'll use for a project, or it can be a number of batches we'll work on per month or quarter.

Overarching Budget

There are situations where we need to consider an overarching budget. While our pace dictates the rate of money spent, an overarching budget helps us prioritize our work.

Fixed projects are more likely to have a budget while ongoing engagements will not. It's nice to have both a pace and budget set, as it allows us to push back on the customer when they ask for more than their budget will allow.

Starting Point

When it comes to figuring out a way to start working with someone, it's usually best to start with a known problem or need. In the cases where the client knows a particular need, we will start by tackling it directly.

Another scenario I face is when the client knows they need help in an area, but they don't know the specific way to get started. In these cases, we launch into our first batch starting with an audit. An audit could include their company, marketing department or their website. The beauty of the audit is it allows us to tackle a problem and adjust as we dive deeper.

Let's recap the BAM system to now include the starting point concept.

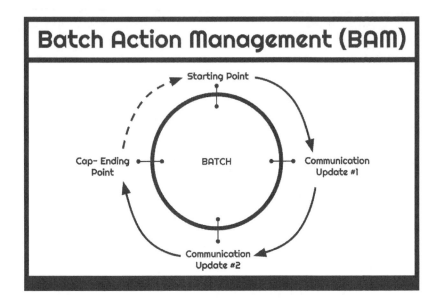

Batch Action Management (BAM)

With BAM, we identify a **STARTING POINT** with our client where we'll list out the actions we want to execute during our first batch of ten hours. Our stopping point (**CAP**) is when we hit ten hours. Our communication check-in points (**Checkpoint**) happen around three and seven hours. The speed (**PACE**) our client decides to work at allows them the ability to control their spend rate.

BAM provides a reasonable amount of updates for course correction and stops the project for re-evaluation systematically. With BAM, there should be no surprises and few mistakes.

Who Is A Good Client In This System?

- Someone who wants clarity while their project is in progress.

- Achievers seeking performance and proactive communication.
- Someone who desires regular entry and exits points while working together.
- Someone burned by vendors who have not delivered on their promises in the past.

BAM In Action

A client hired me to evaluate his website and identify how it was ranking on the search engines. This audit was our starting point. We set up a ten-hour cap with checkpoints at one and five hours. We ran a pace of one batch per week, based on his marketing budget.

In our first hour, I reviewed the website and identified a list of actions we would execute to improve his website search engine rankings. While we continued to work on optimizing his site, I found and documented gaps in the marketing channels, email campaigns as well as the user experience of his company's websites.

In subsequent batches, we tackled these new found marketing actions. Our intent was to go after the lowest hanging fruit and make changes which would improve present tactics while considering future initiatives. Using this organic approach, we were able to increase his rankings, the user experience, and design of his websites all at once. We were also able to establish a more efficient email marketing campaign.

While he was aware of his need for ranking on the search engines, it was the consulting and insight brought through this process which helped his business grow in ways he was not considering when we started. After six batches of work, he had spent his budget, and the exit point in BAM made it easy to pause the engagement. At numerous points in the last few years, we've re-engaged at different seasons continuing each time where we left off before.

With a system for working with clients, let's now dive deeper into discovering our starting points.

Our Starting Points, The Services We'll Offer

When it comes to working as a freelancer, we want to determine what services we're going to offer. We need to resolve which of our skills provide value to our target client.

When I began our marketing agency, I had the ability to produce videos and design websites. It was a natural evolution for me to offer these two services as our company's first offerings.

As our company evolved, we began offering more and better services as customers requested them. We then went through a season where we audited ourselves resulting in us cutting services out and adding new ones altogether.

We won't have it figured out from the beginning, so rest assured there will be opportunities to improve along the way. This on the fly discovery is how it evolved when I began freelancing.

After we had shut down our marketing company, various business leaders reached out and asked for my help solving their problems. They asked for help in areas I was experienced and equipped to serve them.

As clients continued to pay me to help them, I embraced the opportunity to discover what I was best at and most enjoyed.

I'm a communication specialist who helps bring order to chaos. Filtering this down into actionable items resulted in two groups of potential starting points. The first group is business solutions and second is marketing solutions. Four services in each of these two categories, listed next, were what I was best at and enjoyed the most.

Business Solutions	Marketing Solutions
Visioneering: Helping business leaders know and share their vision.	**Joomla Web Design:** Building Semi-Custom Websites.
Organizational Auditing: Providing an objective and insightful picture of an organization.	**Project Auditing:** Identifying a project's opportunities for improvement.
Internal Communication Development: Assisting business leaders bring their teams along.	**Automation:** Streamlining communication with customers.
Leadership Coaching: Helping leaders guide their team.	**Writing:** Crafting communication in a written form.

While it may feel excruciating to trim down everything we can do to just a few services it is important to do so. The more specific we can be, the better. Specific details are great triggers while we're talking with others or when we ask others to refer us.

While I've narrowed my offerings down to these eight starting points, there are additional things I can do for an existing customer, but I'll communicate my skill level or willingness when discussing the project to ensure expectations are properly set.

When operating within BAM (Batch Action Management), our starting points are helpful in getting us going with a customer, but once we're working with a client, we can use SOFI (seeking opportunities for improvement), to illuminate projects for future work together. We'll explore SOFI in the chapter discussing the fourth achievement.

Should I Offer Consulting?
Strategic Versus Tactical Work

When we jump into the world of freelancing, the issue of whether we do strategic consulting work or tactical actions quickly comes to the forefront. While consulting can be profitable and fulfilling, it is also harder to land paid gigs.

When I transitioned from owning a marketing agency to freelancing, I had enough relationships and authority established to generate a healthy dose of consulting work. With numerous projects at a strategic level, it was still not enough to completely sustain us financially. For this reason,

I opted to provide both strategic and tactical services for my clients.

While this turned out to be a prosperous approach, I also found it helpful to execute a variety of work. When fulfilling consulting, there are less tangible deliverables and the work is emotionally heavier because of the stakes involved with those we're impacting.

There are times I've found myself burned out by the weight of consulting, so it's nice to do tactical projects like building a simple Joomla website. It allows me to finish the project and move onto the next adventure. I have a tangible deliverable of something I've created, and this is energizing towards my overall effort. It's a nice balance to have both strategic and tactical projects.

If you're unable to find consulting on the onset but want to make it a part of your offering, place it in the fold of what you can do and look for opportunities with existing clients to extend and fulfill the service. Existing customers who trust you are a great testing ground to explore this new frontier.

For serious consulting consideration, we need to establish ourselves as an authority. To do this, focus on building credibility and authority by actively engaging in social media, blogging, guest writing for other sites and writing books. It does not take much. I've got a friend who consistently posts commentary on news and links through Facebook. With that interaction alone, he has become an authority to his network. We'll explore this further later in the book.

Three Ways To Differentiate

When it comes to differentiating ourselves, there are three surefire ways we can do so with long lasting impact. While some may prefer a short-term differentiator, my preference is for something stronger. Our story (unique journey), our faith (what we believe is possible), and doing hard things are three powerful ways we build a freelancing business that lasts a lifetime. Let's dive into our first differentiator.

Our Story

We all inherited many circumstances we did not choose but are unique to us. Where we came from, the journey we've been on and the lessons we've learned is unique.

Every one of us arrived where we are in life in an entirely different way, and while there are similarities and parallels, there are aspects of our story which no one else shares. Some of these story elements may be beneficial to our currents efforts while others may be completely irrelevant. It is up to us to discover which fall into each category and how we can leverage them to our advantage.

As a freelancer who is a former business owner and a son of a business owner, I have a unique story to connect with my target audience in a way many of my competitors cannot match. This aspect of my story gives me an edge.

One of my past freelancing clients operated a high-end home and kitchen remodeling company. This owner was a former chef who launched a renovation business. What better person to remodel your kitchen than a master of it?

This aspect of his story gives him a unique advantage his competitors can't rival.

Our job as a freelancer is to figure out what our story edge is and share it as part of how we communicate with people.

Let's dive into the second differentiator.

Our Faith & The Vision We Place It In

Believing in something or someone outside our current context differentiates us from others. What we believe in and how strong this faith is will take us far. As freelancers, we want to cast a vision to our clients that we can take them to a place they cannot get to themselves.

Historians asked survivors of the Holocaust what kept them motivated when it was as horrific as it was. The survivors believed the allies would rescue them. Those that lost hope in this rescue died soon after.

In October of 2010 I ran into, now friend, Joe Kissack. Joe is the author of a book called The Fourth Fisherman. If you are unfamiliar with the story, many years ago three Mexican fishermen survived at sea for nine months. They had nothing except a Bible and their faith. In the book, Joe integrated his personal story with the fishermen's amazing story of survival.

In my first conversation with Joe, we talked about how the boat left with five fishermen and only three survived. When I heard this, I immediately wanted to know why some survived and others died. He shared how two fishermen died because they "waited" for rescue and they were unwilling to do the hard tasks needed to live. Waiting for rescue at sea for almost a year without doing anything eliminates any chance of survival. The other three believed they'd be saved, but they also understood they had to do unpleasant things to live long enough for the rescue to arrive.

We must believe we will fulfill our vision for ourselves and our client. There will be times when we must hold true to this belief even when our customers doubt the project's progress.

In many cases, we have faith in ourselves and a client when no one else does. Our faith pushes us beyond what we could imagine, and it has a way of differentiating us from others.

Another practical example of this type of faith is humanity's desire to send a manned mission to Mars. We've never had a human on Mars, and despite the evidence of how difficult this may be, many people believe we can make it happen. When we believe, we will do whatever we can to fulfill this vision. When we lose belief, we lose our vision, and it all fades away. The result, in this case, would be humans never getting to Mars.

On a personal note, I've got faith that God came to earth as a man and then resurrected from the dead. Now whether you believe this or not, it is a powerful belief to know Jesus came back from death. If I believe coming back from the dead is possible, it means I'm either fully committed to what Jesus says or I'm crazy. Thankfully for you, this commitment results in a passion for serving and loving other people.

A strong faith in something or someone greater than ourselves will differentiate us from others. Not many are willing to put their skin in the game to say someone came back from the dead or pay for putting a person on Mars. Those with faith are few, but if that faith aligns, there is nothing that will stop them.

Someone that lacks faith is someone who constantly finds reasons and excuses why we can't accomplish something. These types of freelancers won't last long.

Doing Hard Things

Simply put, people don't like doing hard tasks. Only a fraction of us are willing to push through the difficulty and pain to do it regardless. While doing what is hard is not truly what makes us unique, it will separate us from others.

Take for example the arduous task of climbing Mount Everest. Because of how difficult this is, there is a limited amount of experts who can guide those climbing the mountain. They've differentiated themselves by offering to help people do one of the hardest missions on the planet.

Luckily, as freelancers, we don't have to traverse the difficult physical circumstances of climbing the largest mountains. Doing hard things for us will look much different, but it will require a tough mindset and strong work ethic.

Here are four quick examples of difficult actions we can take to separate ourselves from others.

1. Choosing to hold ourselves to a high level of accountability. Few choose to rise to this level.

2. When we choose to proactively and explicitly communicate, we are elevating ourselves above the competition.
3. Learning to help demanding clients is a rough road where most flee. When I was younger, this task was not only hard but also painful as I was not properly prepared to deal with them. With more experience and maturity under my belt, appropriately dealing with difficult clients has been the catalyst for some of my greatest fruits.
4. Modeling the type of work we offer to our customers publicly in our marketing and operations is the fourth way we can do hard things. The power of reassuring a client by living as an example can be the difference in whether they hire us or not.

While these tactics are effective, they are difficult to maintain, hence the reason they're in the category of doing hard things.

If you adopt these, you'll be a few among many.

What other hard tasks can you do to separate yourself from the competition?

Checkpoint 3 - Our Package Is Published

Knowing what we offer and how we'll work with our clients allows us to publish it online. Whether it is our website, Facebook, Linkedin, or About.me, we want to establish a home base to make it easy for potential clients to see what we have to offer. Start small and embrace the mindset that we can change and expand what we initially post online.

We also want to make it as easy for searchers to find us. If you're not familiar with search engine optimization (SEO), it's helpful to know that every link we get to our website from other sites helps us rank higher for the search phrases we are targeting. Think of it a like a vote and the more votes we get, the more prominently we're displayed. Make sure to add a link to your website or digital home base on all social media profile pages and any place you post your information online.

My first services page simply had two sections, one labeled strategic and the other tactical. Each had a list of services I offered.

Here is what my first iteration looked like two months into freelancing.

"I have spent the last decade bringing my visions to life in the business, political, and entertainment realms. During this season of my journey, I would like to set aside my personal vision and help others bring theirs to life.

Strategically

At a strategic level, I excel in the following two areas:
1. **Chaos To Order** - *Working with an organization to get focused and become effective.*
2. **Content Marketing** - *Orchestrating the creation, curation and distribution of content.*

For existing organizations, campaigns or projects, our starting point will likely be an audit. Click here to learn more about it. For new organizations, campaigns or projects our starting point will likely be a project discovery.

Tactically

At a tactical level, I excel in the following areas:
- *Semi Custom Joomla **Website Design** & Maintenance*
- ***User Experience Design***
- ***Social Media** Marketing (Facebook,Twitter, Pinterest, InstaGram, etc...)*
- ***Content Creation** (Website copy, blogging, Newsletters, etc...)*

If you think working together would help you achieve your goals, please email or call me."

The write-up was simple and straightforward. While you can see it wasn't perfect, it did the job and educated visitors about my offerings.

Seven months into freelancing, I recognized a pattern with how I was helping customers. The first observation was the profile of my clients. In most cases it was the business owner or if it was a non-profit, it was the founder. The second observation was that I helped solve communication problems.

These communication problems fell into two subcategories. First was internal communication, while the second was external (marketing) problems. I decided to restructure my website solutions section to communicate how I helped grow businesses and increase marketing effectiveness.

These two areas would become my focus areas and would be the content of the first conversation between a prospect and myself.

Drilling down to the next layer, I identified starting points within these two focus areas. I knew once I started working with a client on their most significant problem, we'd discover numerous other ways I could help them.

The starting point is usually the hardest sell with a new prospect. With this three-layered system, I'm quickly able to help prospects discover how I could assist them. For those that knew what they need help with, I could now easily let them know If It's in my wheelhouse.

This updated service structure led to the chart you read on page 95 and the framework for how I organized it on my website. [6]When we've deliberately packaged and published our offerings, it makes it easy to share and communicate to others.

By publishing our services publicly it generates a powerful tension for us to monitor it. Ideally, we leverage this pressure to proactively update it as we get a better understanding of it and ourselves.

Now that we're established online let's shift to promoting our personal brand.

---

[6] To see the structure demonstrated, visit www.jasonscottmontoya.com/work

4 OUR PERSONAL BRAND IS PROMOTED

Checkpoint 4 - Our Personal Brand Is Promoted

As a freelancer, we are our brand. We'll succeed at raising awareness of our services based on how well we present ourselves consistently. As a result, we need to present ourselves professionally and as excellently as a company would present themselves.

During my time owning our marketing firm, we found that freelancers had a tendency to disappear on their clients for periods of time or they would communicate poorly throughout the project. This insight was what our marketing company leveraged in the sales process when a prospect was comparing us to a freelancer.

Presenting our personal brand online helps us to prevent this weakness from affecting us. When clients see us active digitally, and they also see us presenting ourselves in a real and personal way. They see someone they can trust and rely on for their projects. Simply put, presenting our personal brand well and consistently helps us establish credibility and rapport over time.

A simple photo and bio on an about page is a good place to start. I've also opted to show my family. Throughout my about page, you get to know me, my purpose, my history, my story, my strengths, personality and showcase projects. The personal brand is about making it easy for people to get to know us. This relational connection will help cultivate trust.

There was someone who reached out to me after following my journey for years, and when we met for the first time, he felt like he knew me. It was great because it allowed us to jump right into his story so I could get to know him.

Remember, like ourselves, our personal brand is a work in progress. We will get to a point in the process where our bio and information is fairly settled. While we strive to get there, let's keep moving and start with what we have. The feedback we'll receive when it's public will help us to refine it for the better. We don't want to get paralyzed because we don't feel we're ready to go live. The secret is to understand that we'll never be perfectly ready to launch.

Once we have our website up and running, it is highly important we realize most people are not going to read it proactively. For this reason, we need to be assertive by meeting people where they are. Bring the elements of our website into the social media channels. To take it even further, share by email, make a phone call or meet with others in-person.

Immediately out of the gate towards landing paying work, I began thinking of creative ideas that others would want to share on my behalf. A medical anatomical diagram came to mind. These types of diagrams show an object in the middle with lines to different parts of the object described in detail.

I happened to have an image of myself cutout from head to toe. Using Google Drawings, I created an image with lines to certain parts of my body. The line going to my eyes had my vision statement. The line to my core muscles listed my core values. The line to my heart listed my passions. Total, eight lines were describing different aspects of who I was. The graphic headlined with my name and had the subtitle, "Strategic Marketing and Communications Specialist"[7].

I uploaded this graphic to my LinkedIn profile and Facebook wall. Because of the creativity and cleverness of the graphic, it was very easy to get others to share it. Fortunately, I had the image of me cut out from a prior project at our marketing company, so I simply added the text and lines. Learning how to leverage the resources we have in front of us is critical to success. *(Feel free to use this idea for yourself)*

Another way I leveraged the resources in front of me was tapping into the thirty-two endorsements others had posted for me on Linkedin. I pulled the top most relevant ones and added the text as an overlay to my portrait photo. These were part of a series of testimonial graphics I created. I would post several different recommendation graphics throughout the month as a way to get exposure and communicate how I could serve others.

While these may seem difficult to make, Google Draw and Canva.com make it easy to do. Both are free, and Canva

---

[7] View the created graphics on PathOfTheFreelancer.com

comes with templates making it easier than ever to create stellar graphics. With tools like these, we don't have any excuses for not professionally presenting ourselves to prospective clients. The bar was raised. Will you rise with it?

A Professional Portrait

A year before we ended our marketing firm I met Keith Taylor, the freelancing friend who wrote the introduction you read at the beginning of this book. After I met him, I was compelled to reach out and discover how I could serve him. This led, from a few extended conversations, to getting together regularly.

He was a full-time freelance corporate photographer, and as an expression of gratitude for my guidance, he offered to do a creative portrait. By this time, I was just about to end the company and start my freelancing journey, so the timing was perfect. I accepted his offer, and we did our photo shoot of the portrait where I'm over pouring orange juice into a cup. This overflow was how Keith experienced me serving him and others. It was his creative vision for communicating that spirit through his craft.

While not everyone will have such an opportunity, we all know a photographer. Either pay them for a professional photo or discover a way to trade work, if you can't afford it. The portrait photo will become part of the foundation for our personal brand, so we want a solid picture.

Business Cards

Coincidently after this portrait was completed, I received an email from a social media influence tool called Klout. Because of the level of influence I had, Klout selected me to receive a perk from a company called Moo. The perk was a set of free business cards from this printing company.

For the front of the business card, I used the newly created portrait. For the back, I had my name, skills, and contact information. I paid the shipping and received my free high-quality business cards. Having this photo on the card created an instant conversation topic while networking. This card helped to break the ice with new relationships.

Company Or Person?

Some freelancers wonder if they should present themselves as an individual freelancer or as a company. Our personal and professional objectives are going to determine which approach helps us achieve our goals more effectively.

When I come across companies that are clearly one individual presenting themselves as a company, it can be off-putting. When I hire a company, I expect to work with a team. When we present ourselves as something different than we are, we face the danger of setting ourselves up for failure.

If you intend to freelance for the long run, I recommend presenting yourself as an individual. If you're planning on building a company, it probably makes the most sense to present yourself as such.

Regardless of which approach you take, articulate the context and expectations for the client, so you set yourself up for success.

Wrapping Up Our Second Achievement

It is a tremendous relief to know how much we want to get paid, to know what we do and how we work with clients, and to publish and promote ourselves with confidence. How well we set the stage in this achievement determines how much time and energy we spend on the following ones.

As we've traversed the second achievement, we reviewed the following four checkpoints that improve how we approach the outside world.

1. Compensation Is Set
2. How & What We Offer Is Defined
3. Our Package Is Published
4. Our Brand Is Promoted

Accomplishing these checkpoints before we jump into freelancing is a huge burden off our back. It makes marketing and selling much easier and more congruent. The shorter the cycle from when someone hears about us and pays us for our first project, the better off we are.

The key is to package our offerings quickly while also refining them into their final state of maintenance where we only need to make small adjustments. With our freelancing structure firmly set, the natural next question is, how do we get clients.

Vital Achievement #3 Steady Stream Of Paying Clients

Getting clients is hard. Getting a steady stream of them can seem impossible. I remember when I first moved to Atlanta and began looking for new client projects. Cold calling was my logical first step, so I made calls to strangers and showed up to storefronts I had never visited. It was intimidating and resulted in many rejections.

If you've done any form of outreach to get new clients as a freelancer, you know what it feels like to face this seemingly uphill battle. The key to attracting prospects is smart consistent activity. To get us there, we'll need to understand how to gain new business, make sales a predictable process, and build a team of advocates. While we can hit the ground running on our own, we'll need help from others to sustain us.

So, where do we start?

① WE'RE FINDING NEW PROJECTS

Easiest To Get New Work — Hardest

Active Clients
Recently Active Clients
Inactive Clients
Prospects & Leads
Connections
Strangers

Sales Type?

Crockpot: Slow & Persistent Over Time

Grill: Quickly Find Need & Push To Solve Now

Checkpoint 1 - We're Finding New Projects

When I first started our Marketing agency, I found my original few clients cold calling. We were living in a city outside Atlanta called Norcross, and they had a business association. On their website, I found a directory of all of the companies in the association, and this became my call list.

Calling through the list, I asked each company if they needed a website. After numerous failed calls, I finally spoke with a business owner that needed a website, and I was excited. They agreed to pay my fifteen-hundred dollar fee, and we met shortly after the call to collect the deposit. Selling my first website was a huge accomplishment, and I felt like I could tackle anything.

While this was a great and unexpected win, I'd come to find out selling to strangers would be the most difficult path to finding new clients.

So, to maximize our efforts to get more business, we'll want to go after the easiest targets first. From my experience and training, I've ordered the easiest targets to the most difficult in the chart below.

1-Active Clients	2-Recent Clients	3-Inactive Clients
4-Prospects	5-Connections	6-Strangers

1-Active Clients

It's always easiest to get more work from active clients. As long as we are doing a good job, there is a need, and they have the budget, our energy getting new work is minimal in this zone. It could be as simple as pointing out an opportunity for improvement and them responding with approval to move forward.

There is a customer I work with who initially committed to two batches (twenty hours) per month. In our second month of working together, he ended up doing five batches for a total of fifty hours.

After the first twenty hours had been completed, he trusted me, saw results and quickly moved forward with new work. This client eventually moved to a commitment of four batches per month after a year of working together.

With active clients, we can ask them what else they need from us or suggest activities based on what we see as ways to help. Either way, if we do good work which produces good fruit, we can expect to get more work from our active clients. Our effort and cost for increased work are smallest for this group.

Get Noticed With Active Clients

People notice excellence, communication, and accountability. I've got a customer who can't quite afford my services, but my level of communication and relational availability for work is precisely what she wanted and needed. So, she finds ways to hire me because what I have is what she most values. At the end of the day, many freelancers can do what I do, but very few offer the insights, accountability, and communication included in my engagements.

2-Recently Active Clients

Clients we've recently worked with have us on their radar. Checking in regularly with these former customers even after we've finished our projects is an excellent way to stay connected. It also maximizes our chances of working together again when future opportunities arise.

When I anticipate a slow week, and can't secure more work from my active clients, I'll first reach out to recently active customers to see what opportunities might be around. When recently active clients have a problem or need, I'll quickly respond and get them moving forward again.

3-Inactive Clients

While they may not have worked with us recently, inactive clients hopefully had a positive experience when they did. Budgets and objectives change, so check back in regularly and see where they may be in the process.

It's great to reach out, check in on the work we did and even send resources which are helpful to them and their team. If we've established an email newsletter, we can ask them to join our list.

These first three groups are our easiest and best chance for getting new work. The longer we've been freelancing, the larger this group will become. Longevity is the beauty of sticking it out as a freelancer. We'll eventually get to a point where our client base is strong enough that we will always have sources of work. Ideally, we've got a line of people waiting to work with us.

Prospects, Contacts & Strangers

When we first start freelancing, and for the first few years, we'll usually end up relying on prospects, contacts, and strangers to receive a sustainable amount of work. Let's explore these three groups starting with prospects.

4-Prospects

Many times potential customers reach out about a project but are not yet ready to pull the trigger. Sometimes those projects are abandoned, or they hire someone else. If they were willing to reach out to us about a project, they're more likely to work with us than a stranger.

When we have downtime, this is a great place to start shaking up new business. Sometimes the projects they asked us about take a long time to start. In fact, many take over a year before they are finally ready to pull the trigger. Be steady, stay connected and follow up. This follow up is our way to secure their business in the future.

One of my freelancing customers and I had known each other before our marketing agency was shut down. Afterward, we got together just as friends to discuss the transition. Eighteen months later, he had a need I could help with and hired me.

Eighteen months may seem like a long time, but sometimes that is how long it might take. We'll want to freelance for the long-run because that is when the juiciest fruit comes to bear.

5-Contacts

Contacts are people we know or have met in some capacity. It could be someone we met at a networking event, a friend from church or a former team member. They are someone we know but has never expressed an interest in working together.

Find people you like and enjoy spending time together. From there, reach out and meet without an agenda. Focus on developing relationships and don't expect actual work ever to come from it. It will produce fruit, but don't go into it for that reason.

There are many great benefits from these relationally focused meetings. I've met new friends, new contacts, and discovered new lessons. For some, it may be weird or awkward just to connect with people on a human level, but when we push through that discomfort, it's powerful.

Share What We've Learned

Learn, learn, learn and never stop learning. With the internet, we won't ever run out of resources for learning. By reading and learning, we can easily share the good stuff with our customers and contacts via email and social media. For broadcasting great content to my network, I use the awesome tool Buffer. I plug in my articles and Buffer throttles the number of links shared each day.

When I come across something that reminds me of a client, friend or contact, I share it with them directly and sometimes privately. Since I am already digging and reading content I value myself, the extra step of sharing is minimal, and its impact is significant.

6-Strangers

Out of all of the groups, it is the strangers who are the least likely to produce new business quickly. While there are exceptions, like when we connect with a stranger at the right time with the solution they need, they tend to require the most energy to get paid work.

On the flip side, sometimes it can be easier talking and selling to a stranger because there are no expectations, no history, and no emotional ties.

While it is a good practice ground to engage with strangers, I'd recommend going after the lowest hanging fruit by starting with active customers and working your way down to the strangers last.

Where To Find Strangers

After starting our marketing company, I did not know what I was doing, but what I did know was I needed to find companies who wanted what we had to offer.

I cold called. I walked into businesses and did whatever I had to do to find interested people. While cold calling was helpful, it was business networking that was a better fit for my personality and approach.

People coming together to meet and connect was something I could get behind. Over the subsequent years, I went to hundreds of networking events meeting thousands of people and winning hundreds of deals for our company. It was fruitful but time consuming.

Cold calling and networking were great sources for clients, but I found referrals were even better. When a client referred another customer our way, it was usually a sealed deal. The sales process was straightforward and easy, and the client was usually someone we valued.

Unfortunately, the process of generating referrals requires time and an active history. Until we have that, cold calling and networking are necessary if we don't want to starve while we grow our freelancing business.

The Grill & The Crockpot

Understanding the stages of our client relationships is helpful so let's shift towards our approach to moving them along in the process.

When it comes to sales, there are two mindsets for driving leads forward. One approach is the Grill Methodology while the other is the Crockpot Approach.

When someone grills food, it includes high heat and flames over a short period to get our tasty meal ready. Thus, the Grill Methodology is the aggressive approach. Here we seek out the need and when we find it, we make our move to persuade the prospect to hire us. We proactively follow up looking for the potential customer and doing everything we can to move them from prospective customer to a paying one.

We are the pursuer, and the client is the big game we're hunting. When we're first starting out, or have a small network, this is the way we'll need approach sales if we're to succeed quickly.

The second way is the Crockpot Approach. The main idea of using a crockpot is to add a bunch of ingredients into a hot stewing pot, and after waiting for hours, the meal is ready. This approach is where we meet people along our journey, and we maintain relationships with them over time. As this relationship develops and a need arises in their world, we become their go-to resource. The dynamic shifts from us pursuing them to prospects seeking us.

Here we are constantly teaching, inspiring and reassuring through our blog, email, social media, phone calls and meetings. We become the expert authority they are looking for when they need it. This approach requires consistency and patience. We'll need to be in it for the long run.

The story of the tortoise and the hare comes to mind. I relate the hare to the grilling follow up process and the tortoise to the crock pot method of selling.

The hare will get us out of the gate and will likely generate significant results, but it will be short-lived. If we want to succeed in the long run, we need to shift from short-term success to long-term sustainability. Over time, we'll learn to leverage both methods depending on our situation.

Filling The Financial Gaps

A great benefit to working as a freelancer, as opposed to running a company, is we only need to provide for ourselves. It only takes a couple of projects to turn our situation around.

When one project ends, for good or ill, the next are right around the corner. Stay optimistic and execute the tasks you need to move forward.

Since we can anticipate there will be times when we've reached out to everyone we could, done everything on our action plan and still not have a client to serve, we'll want to have outlets to fill in the financial gaps. Some income may be better than none.

While it requires we swallow our pride, we must remember no work is "beneath us." In fact, it is this willingness to work "in the trenches" that allows us to move forward during our financial droughts.

There have been times where I've been in survival mode, and I've done work that came my way for ten dollars per hour. In one case, I spent five hours helping a retail store move around their inventory. I heard about the need from our church, and I accepted the call. With no freelancing work slated for that day, my choice was to do this low wage work or do something that would potentially result in a new freelancing gig. Fortunately, in this case, it turned out to be both.

While I was helping the store owner move furniture around, a neighbor retail outlet owner saw me helping. She asked me to help them move their store items around. I accepted, and as a result of that work, I ended up running a garage sale and earning about twenty dollars per hour for planning, promoting and running it.

As a consequence of the garage sale, the owner of the store hired me at seventy-five dollars per hour for thirty hours to build her company a website. My excellent work ethic, our success, and relationship led to her hiring me as a freelance marketer.

Little actions can result in big projects, but it requires we treat our ten dollars per hour job like a seventy-five dollar per hour job to win the rapport and earn the trust we need to get the work we're seeking.

Other Ways To Fill The Gaps

In addition to helping move and run a garage sale, there are other ways to fill in the financial gaps when we have famines. Here is a list of several other ideas to make additional income.

- Movie extra work
- Participate in research and feedback surveys
- Selling our stuff
- Odd jobs, mowing lawns, shoveling snow
- Admin support

When it comes down to it, we've got to pay our bills and sometimes it means buckling down and doing menial tasks to generate enough income to move us forward. This pressure acts as a catalyst towards greater more profitable work.

To minimize the amount of time we spend on these small side jobs, we need to have a sales process and one that generates a predictable income. This is where we're heading in the next checkpoint.

Checkpoint 2 - Sales Is A Predictable Process

After we understand the stages of our customer relationship and how we'll approach them, we can shift our focus to translating a soft skill of selling into a practical break-down with predictable results.

In sales, we have a roller coaster effect of feast and famine. To help alleviate this fluctuation, we want to have a good understanding of how our activity translates into dollars.

Earlier, we identified multiple stages from start to finish for our customer relationship. In the next section, we'll build on that and pull in four of those stages to help us understand how to move people through them.

Transition 1: Strangers To Contacts

To increase the number of connections we have in our digital Rolodex, we'll need to meet an abundance of strangers. This realization also means we need to know how many strangers lead to meaningful relationships.

Transition 2: Contacts to Prospect

With a group of contacts, we next need to determine how many points of contact lead to people interested in our services. Once they transition, they become prospects.

Transition 3: Prospects to Customers

From here, we'll want to identify the number of prospects it takes to establish one paying customer. We also want to track the time it takes for our prospect to turn into a client.

As we pay attention to these transitions in our selling efforts, we'll begin to see a pattern. Here is an example of this playing out.

2 Interactions With 5 Strangers =	4 Meaningful Contacts
3 Interactions With 4 Contacts =	2 Prospects
4 Interactions With 2 Prospects =	1 Customer

This breakdown is providing us a formula for what activity we will need to generate one customer.

1. We need ten interactions with strangers per month.
2. We need to have twelve interactions with our contacts per month.
3. We need to have eight interactions with our prospects per month.

If we do this activity, we'll generate one new customer per month. If we want to get four customers per month, we'll either have to quadruple our monthly activity or become more efficient with moving people from one stage to the next. As we get better and more experienced, the latter will happen organically.

To help us plan further, we'll now estimate our average customer value. Let's say my average customer spends five thousand dollars per year with me. If I want to earn fifty thousand dollars for the year, I'll need to get ten customers. To get ten customers, I'll need to execute the actions listed above ten times.

Since this is not an exact science, and circumstances change things, we'll want to do the extra activity to mitigate against the unknowns. Over time, we'll get a better handle on these unknowns, and we can adjust our operation accordingly.

My time running Noodlehead Marketing gave me the opportunity to build and manage multiple sales processes and teams. This experience provided me the insight to learn the pros and cons of different approaches. While those in business may be familiar with this type of sales breakdown, most freelancers don't even know to think in these terms.

When I verbally shared this analysis with a struggling and stuck freelancing friend, it provided him structure and focus on understanding how he could scale his business and get to the financial destination he was striving towards. It allowed him to realistically see if he could get where he wanted to go or if he needed to change his approach.

While our activity is important, our goal is to build a personal brand where people send us referrals on a regular basis. To do so, we'll need an external team of people helping make our freelance business development easier and more fruitful, which is what we'll explore in the next section.

Checkpoint 3 - We've Built A Team Of Advocates

As freelancers, it can feel like we're on our own, but to succeed we need the help of others. We need mentors, friends, and allies to bring our vision to life.

To succeed at our freelancing career, we'll want to establish a **network of rainmakers** and then **ask for help** when we need it.

Let's Start With Rainmakers

The term Rainmaker has been around in business as long as I've known. The terms refer to someone who attracts customers or brings leads into a business. In the context of our freelance work, rainmakers are our connections who regularly send business our way. They are a source of prospective customers and become our outside sales team.

They know us, and they know other business leaders. When they come across opportunities, we are who they recommend. For us to have rainmakers, it requires we establish trust and reliability with these people, so they know we are a reliable go-to resource for their network. Since it's their reputation on the line, we want to make them look good for referring customers our way by delivering excellent work and communication.

Once we develop several relationships with people we'd deem as rainmakers; it's helpful to track them in our contact management system. When I meet someone who proposes to refer customers my way, or I think they will, I'll label them as a potential rainmaker. When these prospects turn into actual customers, I change their label from potential to proven rainmaker. This tag allows me the opportunity to prioritize and focus on reaching out to these people on a regular basis.

I also ask them to join my email list, connect with them on social media, call them up and meet as much as I am able.

I unintentionally recruited a strong rainmaker advocate doing solid work for one of my customers. My client was using the Hubspot software for marketing automation and website management. The work I had done with this customer was noticed by several people at the company, and their team referred leads my way. Whenever this happened, I sought out the team member and expressed my gratitude for the referral.

The stronger rainmaker network we have, the easier sustaining our freelancing business will become.

Customer Referrals Make Our World Go Round

Like rainmakers, customer referrals are also valuable for sustaining a steady flow of work. When we're focused on maximizing the value we're giving our clients, we'll end up with happy customers. Excited customers love to tell their friends, colleagues, and vendors about our work.

One of the benefits of customer referrals as compared to rainmakers is that it's much easier to maintain and build the relationship as we work alongside them.

With that said, I like to block in my schedule for what I call "community time." At Noodlehead Marketing, we realized there was a time to get work done, and there was a time when it was appropriate to socialize and build relationships.

As a result, we decided to distinctly separate these two purposes by providing community time to our network and clients as a complimentary gift. Sometimes it was simply time before and after a meeting while other occasions it was a meal and hot drinks.

In the business world, I've found these two intentions s get mixed. While sometimes this is not a problem, it can lead to unhealthy habits with lower productivity. We desire relationships, so it's important to make time for them.

Supportive Friends Lift Us Up

Speaking of relationships, the third and last arm of our team of advocates is our friends and family. With rainmakers, they're likely to send us work by way of merit. With friends and relatives, they are likely to send referrals our way as a result of the relationship and care they have for us.

Supportive friends mean easier and quicker referrals. With these referrals, we'll want to steward them with excellence to validate the trust our community has placed in us.

It's unpleasant and problematic to place our community in the awkward position of failed communication or execution. When we do run into issues, we'll want to hold ourselves accountable and seek reconciliation quickly. If our community encourages it, we can invite them to help resolve the issue.

Asking For Help

It takes a lot of humility and the death of our pride to ask for help. We humans prefer to go about it the most difficult way, doing it on our own, instead of involving the help of others.

"Plans go wrong for lack of advice; many advisers bring success." - Proverbs 15:22

While it can be emotionally difficult to ask for help, it's much easier and more productive to work together than on our own. When we're having a slow season and are in need of paid work we can make our situation better faster by reaching out to our closest friends and mentors. Here we'll want to share our situation and what we think we need to get out of it. If we don't know, ask for ideas.

It's most fruitful in these scenarios to ask for specific help like who we need to connect with, what we're looking for, and how they can help. Most people, even strangers are willing to help others. All we need to do is simply ask for it.

Getting Creative From Our Gratitude

When others help us in some way, It's important to express our gratitude for their support. For me, it tends to be a simple thank you note to express my gratefulness. In other cases, I'll buy someone a meal as an expression of thankfulness.

I recently referred a client I'm working with to another friend and social media freelancer Toby Bloomberg. She's super talented at her craft and one of the gentlest spirits I know. Anytime I get a chance; I love to refer people her way. As a result of my recent referral she went and purchased a gift basket for my family and me with all kinds of breakfast goodies.

It does not take much to make a great impression. Expressing our thankfulness, in a culture that tends to lack it, speaks loudly about our character. It cultivates a long-term harvest and leads to a state where people seek us out for the work we do.

Checkpoint 4 - Referrals & Leads Seek Us Out

The ending of Noodlehead Marketing led to a flurry of people reaching out to me. They wanted me to help them before I decided what I was going to do next vocationally.

In the first two years of freelancing, almost all the work I did was from people I knew and referrals from those I worked with in the past.

Jumping into freelancing, I thought I'd have to hit the ground running to generate contacts and leads. Thankfully God's provision, in response to my faithful stewardship of relationships over the years, was ready to bear fruit in a powerful way.

Activities That Lead To More Work

While much of the work at the beginning of my freelancing journey was a result of the vacuum created by the company shut down, the fact they continued flowing my way was a result of behaviors I maintained in the years beforehand.

Maintaining relationships without agendas may not lead to work in the short term, but I've reaped a harvest in the medium and long-term.

There was one friendship where a freelancer took a full-time job with a company, and he referred his clients my way because he trusted I would take care of them in his absence.

Doing great work leads to referrals. When we've established a reputation and authority in an area, people seek us out to help them solve their problems.

One such example was the result of my excellent project execution early in my freelancing journey. This small project led to a much larger one when this person decided to launch their company.

Whether small or large, we want to take our work seriously and deliver each project as if it's our most important one.

We never know who is watching or what it will lead to in the future.

Simple Activity Leads To Work Over Time

I've mentioned before about establishing and promoting our personal brand. This essential step helps us create authority, build credibility and simply remind people we exist.

Three months before I began freelancing, I was blogging three times per week. Since I was also finding and reading great content, I'd share this on my blog, Facebook, Twitter, and Linkedin. While the blog writing took time, the content sharing took very little since I was already in the habit of reading tons of great online content.

Five months of freelancing and I realized Noodlehead Marketing had an email list I could leverage. We had used the list to communicate the shutdown, follow-up on the status of the team members and as part of a campaign to help launch my freelancing career.

Grateful to inherit this list of about eight-hundred people, it gave me another platform to nurture potential freelancing opportunities.

I set up a system to read content (Feedly), mark for sharing (Pocket), and then share (Buffer) on my social media accounts. Using Mailchimp, I set up an RSS email campaign, so a weekly email digest was sent with my latest blog posts. This process of sharing content and promoting my blog posts made it easy to build authority and remind people of my existence.

The email list became a great channel to invite contacts, prospects, and clients into the fold. It also allowed me to stay in touch with numerous people efficiently. Outside of email collection on the website, personal invites to the list is the primary source of its growth.

When it comes to blogging, I've tried different formats and lengths and each season requires something different. When I first started blogging, I would create a graphic asking a compelling question every Monday. On Wednesday, I'd create a blog post with the best content I found during the past week. On Friday, I'd post a personal story or leadership insight.

For several months, I was posting three times per week regularly, but it was hard to maintain once my paid workload increased. As it did, I shifted towards posting a few times per month but posting something long. This change was great because I'd put a lot more energy behind promoting them and driving traffic.

Unfortunately, these posts are mentally much tougher to think about, draft and publish. As my workload continually increased, I decided at the beginning of 2016 to shift towards quick short form blog posts a few times per week. These posts were less than a few hundred words each, but they were quick to create and had takeaways for the busy reader.

In conversing with others, I realized I was thinking through and challenging many insights in these conversations. New and refined ideas, as well as many epiphanies, came through these conversations. I captured these insights and spent ten to fifteen minutes writing them into a short, simple blog post. While writing this book, I dropped down to a monthly blog write-up.

Don't feel like you have to follow a specific guideline. Instead, adapt your approach to your context. When we have little-paid work, we can easily devote time to these online promotional activities. The key is to maintain a small level of activity to ensure our flow of work continues even when we have an abundance of clients.

Consider Donating Time

When we don't have enough paid work to fill our hopper, it's a good time to explore volunteering. While many freelancers are inclined to give away speculation work to companies as part of an attempt to earn their business, I believe it is much more fruitful and meaningful to intentionally give away our talents to a non-profit organization that can benefit from our efforts. We also benefit by getting the experience, building our portfolio and establishing a relationship that could lead to future client referrals.

In my first year of freelancing, I volunteered for a local Christian men's group. I put together and moderated a panel of three specialists to talk about how fathers can provide a safe technology experience for their children. As a result of this volunteer effort, an audience member hired me and several of my freelancing friends to help them launch their new company.

If you're inclined to help others regularly, consider building into your work life a standard allotment of hours per month or year you're willing to give away. Make sure to set a cap on free work, trade work, and business equity work. While giving or trading our time can be worth it in the right context, we want to make sure we don't starve while we wait for the fruit of these long-term partnerships.

Wrapping Up Our Third Achievement

Creating a steady stream of clients is a huge milestone in our freelancing journey and one which requires perseverance. As we close out the chapter, let's review the four checkpoints we've passed on our journey.

1. We're Finding New Projects
2. Sales Is A Predictable Process
3. We've Built A Team Of Advocates
4. Referrals & Leads Seek Us Out

The beauty of freelancing is we need only provide enough work for ourselves. I remember the days of having a team of people and having to earn twenty to thirty thousand dollars in a month just to cover expenses and payroll. That was an enormous responsibility to carry and one I did as the primary salesperson.

To generate the business, we need to survive and thrive as a freelancer; we need to build up a network of people that help us do the heavy lifting and get to a state where we do little to no sales for generating new paid projects.

Once we've got a flow of referrals transforming into active customers, our next focal point shifts to maximizing these client engagements.

Vital Achievement #4 Active Clients Are Maximized

With prospects flowing our way, many will transition into paying clients. With an abundance of clients we can easily miss a low hanging fruit opportunity. From my personal experience and observation of others, maximizing active customers is one of the most neglected areas of growth.

In my past business, I would sell a deal and move onto the next one without appreciating the lost potential in doing so. Since active clients have the most readily available income potential, it's important we create a mutually sustainable working relationship. Think about ourselves and the client as sponges. Our task is to wring out the water. We give all the value we can within the needs and budget.

While we're providing value working with clients who trust us, we have the opportunity to build a passive income stream. Passive income seem less profitable, but it is vital to long-term growth and steadiness.

Once we have an abundance of clients we've maximized and they are working with us on an ongoing basis, we then work towards only engaging with ideal clients. But, before we get too ahead of ourselves, the first step in this direction is sustaining client relationships.

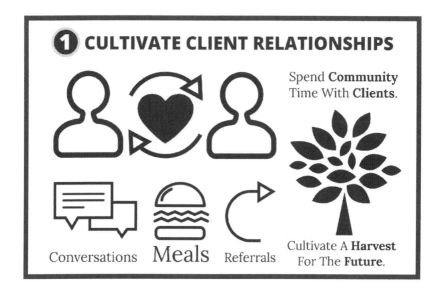

Checkpoint 1 - Cultivate Client Relationships

Sustaining meaningful relationships as a freelancer is critical to our success. Doing so with our clients will elevate the mutual commitment. No matter how great we are at what we do and how we work with our clients, there will always be situations where problems and tensions arise. It is during these moments we'll want a healthy relationship in place to encourage our clients to push beyond these issues.

When we're focused on surviving as a freelancer, we'll lean towards short-term and emotional reasoning. In this state, we are more likely to focus on extracting value from others instead of giving it. At the moment it seems like a productive route, but it usually leads to quick wins and long term losses.

Building a freelancing business for the long term is like us tending a garden. Our role as the gardener is to plant seeds and nurture them, but there is nothing we can do to force the plants to grow. Some relationships will bloom into clients, but in other cases they'll refer clients our ways. Other times we'll find new friends or someone we can help.

Immediately after shutting down my business, I had an acquaintance request a lunch with me. We spoke and began a new and fruitful relationship. After a year of getting together as friends sharing business stories, he hired me to help him with several of his company's projects. We worked together for a few months until the project concluded. Afterward, his company became a valuable vendor resource for several of my customers.

We never know where our relationships will go, but if we jump into them authentically, we'll find they are well worth our time. It also requires we care for and nurture our relationships beyond our desire to win business.

We're limited by the time and energy we have available. Building relationships require an abundance of both. I've found it helps to cultivate and sustain relationships by providing value in ways that naturally align with how I operate my life.

Three ways I organically build up these friendships is by connecting people together, referring prospects, and sharing relevant resources. These are activities I do with no expectation of reciprocation.

When I first arrived in Atlanta, I knew almost no one in the area. Within three to four years, I had networked with nearly ten-thousand people. With so many connections, acquaintances and friendships, I built a network that easily allows me to find connections between people regularly.

When I find people who can help each other personally or professionally, I get excited about connecting them. Sometimes it can be a prospect searching for a friend's services while other times it can be a friend who can empathize with the other's life situation.

While I don't seek out financial benefit for this effort, it's a behavior that builds long-term trust in the relationship. A strong friendship leads to a strong support system which we'll explore further, in the fifth achievement. When there is not professional fruit, I'm content with an outcome that leads to the personal growth for me or those in my community.

Lastly, I love to share valuable resources. Videos, articles, links, blogs, and podcasts are things I'm always exploring. When they are excellent or when they resonate with me in a personal way, I'm quick to share with my network or with individuals that come to mind.

By constantly sharing these resources on my blog, social media and directly with those I think would benefit the most, I'm helping to maintain relationships and establish awareness of my existence and activities.

Sharing links with others is an easy and valuable way for me to stay connected with people. Another variation of this is sharing entertainment related content such as music videos. I usually listen to Pandora when I'm working, and certain songs and tunes remind me of people. Instead of holding onto the memory, I share it with the person that comes to mind so we can enjoy the connection together.

However you decide to do it, cultivate those relationships and the garden will produce a harvest in ways we expect and many where we're pleasantly surprised.

② PASSIVE INCOME STREAMS

Chose **High Impact, Low Effort** Options.

Find **Passive Income Stream** Opportunities.

Numerous Small Amounts **Over Time** Generate **Significant** Income.

Checkpoint 2 - Passive Income Streams

During the days of running our marketing firm, we offered to host our client's website for twenty five dollars per month. Unfortunately, we were selling websites for thousands of dollars, so the small amount of income seemed unimportant. As a result, we didn't prioritize selling this and other small monthly services to our clients because we were so focused on the large ticket items.

I reflected on this and realized we had missed a tremendous income opportunity. Over the course of our business, there were one-hundred companies we could have sold our twenty-five dollars per month hosting. One-hundred companies paying twenty-five dollars equals $2,500/month. This revenue is $30,000/year. This insight is when I realized how important it was to build a passive income stream. Not only does it allow us to stay connected to our clients, but it also generates a sizable and relatively easy to manage revenue.

Every dollar counts, especially when they are recurring dollars. As a freelancer, our income potential is capped by the number of hours and projects we can work at one time. Passive income allows us to go beyond that cap and help buffer us when work is slower. Learn from my mistake and take this checkpoint seriously as early as possible.

Identify Opportunities For Passive Income

To sell passive income services, we need first identify which ones we'll offer. This process starts be ideating on services we could provide that would require minimal effort and provide significant value. We'll also want to identify ideas that compliment the main services we offer.

As I entered into freelancing, I adopted two of the services we offered for our marketing company and then invented a third option. The two adopted services were website hosting and the second was consolidated marketing reporting services through the tool, Agency Analytics.

This marketing reporting tool tracks keywords on search engines and brings in Google Analytics and social media insights into one consolidated report. There are very few customers that have these type of reporting and keyword tracking, so most clients I work with are prime candidates to use the service. Also, the marketing reports provide great insights that I can leverage for making future improvements in their digital efforts.

With experience as a reseller website host, the option to continue charging twenty-five dollars per month for website hosting was a no brainer. Unfortunately, in many cases, companies already have a hosting company, and since I'm not the cheapest, I can't rely on every client utilizing my service. Since I'm not in the hosting business, I also don't want to compete on price. As a way to respond to this reality, an idea came to mind for a third service of how I could help my hosting clients as well as those who already have a hosting service in place.

Hacking and website attacks have increased recently, and it made sense to offer an update, backup, and security package. The focus would be to prevent any attacks, but in the event it happened, we'd be prepared to restore a backup quickly. This service became the third passive income I'd offer to my clients.

Here is how the three services break down regarding income generated.

Website Hosting	Consolidated Marketing Reports	Backup & Update Security Package
$25/month	$25/month	$50/month

For every client I work with, I now have one-hundred dollars per month or twelve-hundred dollars per year of potential passive revenue. While it is rare that a customer will use all three services at once, I'll usually get a client to at least proceed with one of the three options. With a relationship built on trust, the sale becomes relatively easy and quick.

Two and half years in, I had about seven-hundred dollars in recurring passive income per month which results in a little over eight-thousand dollars per year. My goal is to increase recurring revenue every year by three-hundred dollars per month. This increase will provide me with more time to work on my side projects and to focus on non-work related activities I want to invest in personally.

Checkpoint 3 - Ongoing Client Engagements

Most clients will want to work with us when they have a known specific problem we can help them solve. This knowledge results in a one and done project that, when complete, ends the relationship. Since existing customers are our best source of new work, it's best we set ourselves up for an ongoing engagement even while working on these projects. One way to accomplish this is by proactively documenting how we can help them once we've completed our current tasks, enter SOFI.

Seeking Opportunities For Improvement (SOFI)

SOFI is a proactive drive to discover opportunities for improvement while we're working on approved projects. It is critical for long-term success as a freelancer. It also helps increase the value provided to our clients. While a customer won't always want to address them at the moment, when they do, we'll have the next project lined up before we finish the current one. Business leaders also love the proactive nature of this activity.

Those who are more experienced will easily see opportunities for improvement while we're working on an existing project. The key is not to just notice them and move on, but instead to document them. I've recorded these on a simple notepad, spreadsheet and in the software tool Trello. For more detailed and complex scenarios, I'll use Airtable to make sense of the chaos.

This documentation is important for when we communicate our updates to clients of what is going on and what we recommend working on next. With the tools in place, we'll need an effective system for how to capture and process these ideas. The framework I use is called IDEMA[8].

---

[8] IDEMA is a framework for capturing and sustaining ideas. IDEMA is a Creative Commons license. Learn more at https://medium.com/@IDEMA

Meet IDEMA. It's How We'll Organize Our Actions

Understanding how we will work with a client is helpful. The next important factor is understanding how the actions are organized while we work with our customers and their vendors.

A few years back at Noodlehead Marketing, we faced a big problem. We needed a strong project manager, but it was our "white whale", elusive as ever.

We thought we had a project management problem, but we were dealing with a separate issue. We lacked order which prevented the "right" type of person from seeking out our company. When they did come into our organization, they'd leave because they felt like we operated as "cowboys" in the "wild west." It was a chicken and egg situation. We believed we needed a project manager, but our mess was keeping them from staying. We had to work on ourselves before we could attract and retain the type of team member we needed.

After churning through several people, we buckled down and decided to build a system to resolve the root problem. We sliced project management horizontally instead of vertically. For us to do this, we needed to establish a system and we began asking ourselves to identify what process every internal and external project went through.

We came up with a framework called IDEMA. It is a framework for capturing and sustaining ideas. It's a filter for excellence and accountability. It was the path we realized every idea went through. Here is the IDEMA framework.

1 - Ideate - Capture Our Idea.
2 - Discover - Establish Intentions & Plan To Sustain.
3 - Execute - Start, Finish & Prepare To Maintain.
4 - Maintain - Sustain Our Idea.
5 - Audit - Determine Our Assessed Idea's Fate.

There are two starting points we can take when using this framework. The first is to use it with new ideas. We capture the concept and describe it enough to know what it is when we refer to it. From there we need to discover the idea by planning it out, identifying resources and roadblocks and assigning responsibility.

Once it's created, we slide the idea into maintenance where we sustain the idea over time. At some point, we'll audit the idea to improve, keep as-is or to terminate it.

The second scenario we'll use IDEMA is when we've got an existing idea or project we need to move forward. Here we'll identify where the idea should belong within the five stages and once we place it, we'll move it forward from there.

Each of our personal contexts will determine which approach we ought to use for our clients when seeking out opportunities for improvement (SOFI). Starting from the beginning, Ideation, is always easiest as we simply follow the process mapped out. It's when we're thrown into the middle of the process that things can get chaotic and messy.

In the middle of 2013, my wife was burnt out and pregnant with our third child. She needed help, and I was willing to give it. I wanted to spend an hour with her discovering how I could help her, but unfortunately, she was so tired, she felt she could not tell me how I could help her. At the time, she was also resistant to my help.

I faced two challenging roadblocks. The first was someone who needed help but couldn't tell me how to help them, and the second was someone who needed help but was resistant to receiving it. For my clients, this is a common occurrence, so it was an opportunity to learn for future work application.

While I preferred to follow the IDEMA process from beginning to end, I had to set aside my preferred way of doing things and instead start from the end, with the audit.

To help my wife, I began with ideas I knew would help her and would be difficult to resist. My first step was to get up early in the morning with the children, get them ready, and make them breakfast. Telling her she could sleep in while I took care of the kids would be hard to resist and it was. I mean, would you say no to this?

So, this became my starting point.

From there I began writing down every action that had to get done for our family and home. These actions included cleaning, groceries, and personal finances. By the time I finished, I'd combed through everything.

As I collected actions, ideas, and projects, I placed them into one of the five stages of IDEMA.

Ideate	Discover	Execute	Maintain	Audit

As I began to do this, many of them were related, so I grouped actions into projects.

This process is also similar to how I help our young children clean their rooms. With toys, clothes, dishes, and garbage everywhere we first move it all into a pile in the middle of a room.

We then begin by finding all of a particular type of item. It could be blocks or clothes, but something specific. We find all of them and place them into their container. If there isn't a container, we'll create one. We then go through each category until our pile is empty.

For our household, our kids or business, this process transforms something that seems overwhelming and makes it easier to address. We place chaos into the IDEMA machine and out pops organization, order, and focus.

Like my wife, many of the business owners I've worked with while freelancing are burned out and tired. Their operations are moving forward, but they are tangled in chaos.

While helping them to address immediate needs and problems, I simultaneously organize their efforts into this framework. This organizational process results in a blueprint for where they've delegated their authority my way.

By actively seeking opportunities for improvement (SOFI), clients constantly see how I've helped them in the past, how I assist them today, and how I can help them tomorrow. When customers decide to slow down or stop their working relationship with me, it's usually financial in nature, not because of a lack of need. For many clients, I'm able to generate an abundance of results to help fund their expense in hiring me, and it becomes a foregone conclusion to continue.

Working within the IDEMA framework also provides a mindset where we start with the end in mind. There will be a point where one or both of us will decide to part ways, and I want to ensure that when it happens it is a seamless transition and one which results in celebration, not turmoil.

IDEMA, In summary

While there are many great systems for working on projects, this is the system I believe best works within my strengths, weaknesses, and personality. The beauty of people is we are different and have different ways of doing things. If IDEMA is not a good system for you, consider checking out Agile or Waterfall. There is no shortage of project management systems to help you achieve at a higher level.

At the end of the day, what matters most is you have a good system, not that you use IDEMA. In fact, feel free to take aspects of IDEMA or any other system and construct a new methodology.

Four Practical Ways To Give Value And Get More Paid Work

We want to make our client relationships better and get paid to provide value. I've found the following four simple, focused and meaningful strategies make the places and lives of those we work with better.

Ask How We Can Help

To help serve our clients, let's ask them what they need or want and how we can help them accomplish it. When it comes to working with new customers, they know more about their business and what they need than we do.

For this reason, I tend to ask clients what they need help with and start our work engagement there. As I work with them in the areas they've asked for help, I observe and document other opportunities that we can shift to once we've completed our starting point projects. I've also found it fruitful to check in with clients weekly to see what additional help they need.

Eagerly Respond To A Client's Request For Help

In our effort to serve others, let's establish in our minds a willingness to help them or clearly communicate when we can't. When we're engaged in work with someone who has a hard time asking and receiving help, it is of particular importance to respond to the ask eagerly. We want them to feel safe asking, and we want to be honest when we can't or need to delay our support.

Use Our Opportunistic Eyes

In moments it can be obvious, although not always convenient, how we could help someone. When it's the small things, there is little risk and time involved in helping them. When we see something that can be fixed, updated or resolved quickly and we've got an established relationship, we can opportunistically help while we're doing what we're doing. We're simply piggybacking on the energy of our current task to help.

I'm checking out valuable content daily on a variety of topics. Many times these topics touch on issues, problems, and opportunities my clients are currently facing. It's an easy few clicks to share this insight with them, but it can have a tremendous impact on the relationship and their context. In some cases, it provides ideas for new ways we can work together.

Proactive And Systematic Help

When it comes to things we know are needed and cherished by our client, let's commit to taking care of the observed but unmet responsibilities. I tend to primarily engage with business owners who are busy running their company, managing people and juggling many different responsibilities at once. When they've committed to a budget for my services, I pro-actively identify how and when we'll direct our efforts. Simply put, I make it as easy as possible for them to work with me and help grow their business.

When we're asking how we can help, eagerly responding to the ask, jumping opportunistically on ways to serve, and systematically helping, we'll sustain an active and healthy client relationship. Our grateful clients will want to continue working with us and likely expand the budget over time.

Strategic Maximization Of Client's Hours

As freelancers, we'll work with a handful of clients at any given time. I continue to evaluate my clients, their needs and how engaged they are to determine how I pace myself in working through the hours they've approved. With a monthly goal for the number of hours I'd like to log for paying clients, I want to schedule it out in a way that maximizes my chances to accomplish my target.

For customers who commit to a certain number of batches per month, I work on knocking those hours out as quickly as possible while also leaving some time to address any actions that I may need to do unexpectedly. Finishing these hours first gives me the opportunity to work on other client projects, and it also gives customers a chance to do more hours if and when they need it. One client, I started working with committed to twenty hours, which was two batches per month in the BAM system. Because of our quick success we ended up doing five to six batches (Fifty to sixty hours) for the following three months.

Some customers are not engaged with the work I do, and they give me free reign to do what I want when I want. I'll work these clients around the ones with a more structured expectation. When our scheduled clients are busting at the seams of our calendar capacity, we've now got the leverage to start filtering our customers into the sweet spot, the final checkpoint for this achievement.

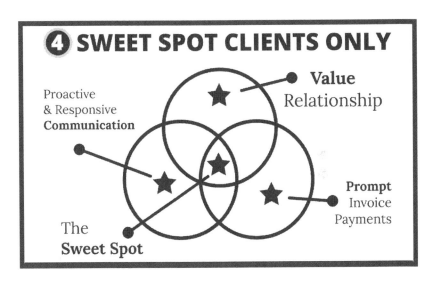

Checkpoint 4 - Sweet Spot Clients Only

We will all work with demanding clients. It was one, in particular, I was struggling with that led to a discussion with a fellow freelancer. I had finished twenty hours of work for this client, and he was late to pay the fifteen hundred dollars. On top of the overdue payments, his communication throughout the ordeal was late, inadequate, or absent.

When it came to collecting payment, I was constantly emailing, calling and texting about it for six weeks until I finally received all fifteen hundred dollars.

My experience with this client was stressful, and I did not enjoy working with him. After we had finished the twenty hours, the customer came back to communicate I was not worth what I charged and tried to get me to provide a lower hourly rate. For all the hoops he wanted me to jump through, it was not worth me changing my system to accommodate this client. If I'm going to accommodate anyone, I'd rather it be my great clients, not my terrible ones.

Around the same time, another company was referred my way. After meeting with this referral, we hit it off immediately. While I was working on the project, she was great in her communication, and she also paid early. By all accounts that mattered to me, she was the opposite of the first client.

As a result of these two dynamically different scenarios, I developed a client quality rating system to help me build a book of business consisting of great customers.

- Do they pay early, on time or late?
- Do they communicate poorly, average, or great?
- Do I value working with them? Yes, or no?

If I can answer all three of these for a client positively, they are a sweet spot client. If they are late, a poor communicator and I don't value working with them; they are the lowest quality client I can have.

As a freelancer with an abundance of work, the goal is only to have sweet spot clients. The more leads we generate and active projects we have on our plate, the easier it is to let go of the poor quality customers and only work consistently with great ones.

Managing An Abundance Of Paying Clients

You may be in the midst of it or may wonder if it will ever happen, but if you stick it out, there will come a time when there is too much work to handle. Two and half years in and this was the state of my freelancing. By this point I had referrals flowing my way, clients were maximized, and I had more work on my plate then I had time to fulfill. I was also actively referring leads to fellow freelancers and friends, and it was after I increased my hourly rate from seventy-five to eighty dollars per hour.

My wife and I also set a goal to buy a house at that time, so the influx of work was a welcome increase in activity. To lean into this income opportunity, I changed my daily end time from five thirty PM to six thirty PM. This increase provided an extra hour per day, five per week and twenty-two per month.

While this abundance of work was a great problem to have, I was stressed and overwhelmed by it. By the end of August, I had logged thirty hours above my normal monthly paid hour cap of 128.

Immediately after this sprint, I was burnt out. In fact, I had to delay working with one new client and say no to another prospect who wanted to work with me because of how much was on my plate.

Worn out with another high volume month ahead of me, I had to setup a simple way for me to finish my week while also leaving behind any feeling of being overwhelmed when I entered the weekend. I also wanted to ensure my clients were satisfied. While much of the work I'm involved in does not have hard deadlines, I still wanted to move tasks forward.

So, I modified my weekly check-in to address this. I'd let the customer know what I was working on for the week. In my freelancing dashboard in Airtable, I created a field to list my week's goals and a way to filter them based on completion. This method allowed me to knock out the goals early in the week and use the remaining days to work on less important items.

This process also resulted in me completing my top priorities at the beginning of the week as well as getting a ton of secondary items finished. By week's end, I'd feel great about my progress and clients were happy their important tasks were complete.

Another piece of the puzzle was scheduling out my time to work out the number of hours each client committed to for the month. In my dashboard, I added a pace of hours I need to log daily to complete the number of hours for each client individually and for all of them collectively. Easily, I could now see how realistic it was for me to finish the number of approved hours for the month.

With these two changes in place, I now see my top priorities and how many hours I need to work for each client. Addressing my root feelings of being out of control and overwhelmed are now gone, and I can enjoy my weekends with family.

Wrapping Up Our Fourth Achievement

Since active clients are our best opportunity for increasing our income and establishing financial security, this achievement is key to creating an established and steady freelancing vocation. Let's review the four checkpoints we've hit along the way.

1. Cultivate Client Relationships
2. Passive Income Streams
3. Ongoing Client Engagements
4. Sweet Spot Clients Only

When we master this achievement, we'll come to realize that we've tapped into revenue sources that could financially provide for decades. Imagine getting to this place and only working with sweet spot clients.

Yes, it's sweet to ponder :-)

Now, with feast comes the inevitable famines, so our next question becomes, how do we survive and thrive when income goes up and down?

Vital Achievement #5 Unaffected By The Roller Coaster

It is stressful beyond imagination to live by the tension that comes from the ups and down of the roller coaster. One day we feel like a million bucks while the next we wonder if we should even continue to exist.

I remember the dread I experienced knowing the lives of my team and their families were dependent on my ability to generate enough paid work to run payroll. Every month became an uphill battle to survive. By the end of the month, I was beaten up and burnt out only to have to start the whole process over again when the new month began.

Consistency in income and workload is our goal, but as freelancers, we're going to experience seasons of feast and famine. During times of plenty, we'll want to manage our resources so we can live well when we're receiving little to no income.

Our first step to accomplishing this is to have a plan in place of how we'll respond when income dries up. When it does, we're able to respond swiftly and thoroughly. Let's start planning.

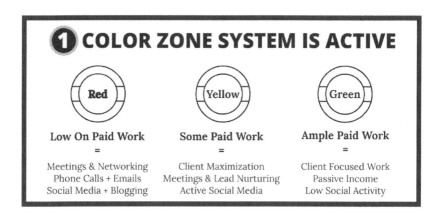

Checkpoint 1 - Color Zone System (CZS) Is Active

Expecting seasons of high activity and times when we have no work is one way to think of the roller coaster. It's also helpful to think of these two states as times of war and times of peace. To survive and thrive we'll want to change how we act during these two entirely different contexts.

A Color Zone System (CZS) in place will enhance our chances of success and minimize our times of panic, but we need to determine how we'll respond beforehand so when it gets bad, we don't panic.

CZS is a visual way to accomplish this. As mentioned earlier in the book, this is the deeper dive into how the three color zone system works.

Years ago a friend gave me a book, Execution Without The Drama by Patrick Thean, which talked about a system revolving around these three colors. Based on the color, individuals, departments and the company would respond according to predetermined plans. Everyone knew how they were to execute when the context changed.

When I began freelancing, I knew the roller coaster ride of feast and famine was coming, and I wanted to do whatever I could to mitigate against this dynamic from the beginning because of how draining it is over time. To accomplish this, I developed a RED, YELLOW, GREEN system for how I would behave based on what color zone I was in.

There are two measures for the zone. The first is the number of hours I've slated for the week, and the second is the amount of income I received for the month. One gives me vision on my status while the other provides direct insight on the actions I need to take now.

Color Zones Based On Income Received

RED	YELLOW	GREEN
Less Than $5,000/Month	Between $5k-$7k/Month	More Than $7,000/Month
Less Than $1,176/Week	Between $1,176-$1,647/Week	More Than $1,647/Week

Color Zones Based On Hours Secured

RED	YELLOW	GREEN
Less Than 68 Hours/Month	Between 68-93.5 Hours/Month	More Than 93.5 Hours/Month
Less Than 16 Hours/Week	Between 16-22 Hours/Week	More Than 22 Hours/Week
Less Than 3 Hours/Day	Between 3-4.5 Hours/Day	More Than 4.5 Hours/Day

In the red zone, I have little-paid work but lots of time. My set of actions for the RED zone is heavily weighted towards relationships, sales, and marketing to generate paid work. These activities include meetings, calls, emails, and high levels of online activity.

In green, it means I have an abundance of paid hours but little time to promote myself and cultivate relationships. My set of actions for green is focused on client work. Green also leads to maintaining some relational and promotional activities, so when my projects are finished, I'll have a pipeline to work.

Here's a table with the some of the actions each zone contains. There are other actions included on my full list, but this will give you an idea of how you could shape your action plans for each zone.

Action Description	Red Zone	Yellow Zone	Green Zone
Pray, thank God for his provision	X	X	X
Work on paid client work	X	X	X
Billing & invoices	X	X	X
Share articles on social media with Buffer	Daily	Weekly	Monthly
Publish a new blog post	4/month	2/month	1/month
Meet with people	5-8/week	3-4/week	1-2/week
Seek business from existing and recent customers	X	X	

Drive leads forward	X	X	
Guest blog on other websites	X	X	
Send articles to network	X		
Do side jobs	X		

With a strategy of doing great work in place, we can expect our clients to work with us over an extended period as well as referring people they know our way. This strategy also makes it easier for us to stay in the green zone.

On the flipside, we want to be sure to keep some of our sales and marketing efforts online when we are in the green zone, so we don't appear to others that we've disappeared off the planet. This silence can make our lives more difficult when the famine comes back our way.

Also, it's wise to set a cap on the number of hours we intend to work in a month to prevent our work from overtaking our lives. We'll talk more about unifying our personal and professional lives in the seventh achievement. My hour cap is 128. While there may be exceptions, this cap sets a clear boundary to help me guard my personal life. When I go over it, a flag is raised, and a discussion is needed.

How To Know Our Zone

To know what zone we're in, we need to track our income and number of hours. In the next chapter we'll talk about tools to help us track this, but for now, we'll explore four categories of income we want to keep an eye on. The four categories include collected money, invoices, unbilled work and anticipated work.

Collected Money is cash received and deposited into our bank account. This is the most important number in determining where we stand for the month.

Invoices are the amount of money we've billed clients for. In most cases, I invoice on the start of each ten-hour batch to be due within ten days of the invoice creation. I prefer this method because it allows me time to complete the work and receive payment by the time I've finished.

Unbilled Work is billable hours we've not yet sent an invoice for. In these cases, I'll create a draft invoice for this time when I'm tallying the total for unbilled work. In addition to providing visibility, this action makes it quick and easy to send the invoice when I've completed the project.

The top three categories above are the most important numbers because they are real income. Except for rare cases when a client does not pay us, we can anticipate the money will come.

Anticipated Work is work we think we'll receive at some point in our current month. To help us plan ahead, monitoring this category of income is helpful. I have clients who let me know they plan to work with me for a specified number of batches per month. This helps me to estimate potential income ahead of time. When a client has not committed to work, but they have a track record of monthly hours, I'll consider it in this category as well.

The more accurate our numbers are in this window, the wiser decisions we make when planning our months, accepting new clients and knowing when to raise our rates.

Actual Versus Potential Hours

In addition to tracking income to help measure what zone I'm in, I also track the number of billable hours, so I know how much more I need to achieve a green week and month.

I'll generate weekly hour tallies to add in my freelancing dashboard. This dashboard resides inside Airtable and is where I also track each month's hour total. This type of tracking, which I did not implement until a year after freelancing, allows me to see patterns and identify opportunities for improvement. It also allows me to see where I'm heading and how to change my behavior to create a different result.

In addition to tracking approved hours, I also track potential hours. When I run out of actual hours, I focus on moving potential hours into actual hours. When I've exhausted these efforts, I concentrate on generating new work.

With my dashboard, I attempt to answer the following three questions. How many billable hours do I have for today? The week? The month?

Recently I had a lead reach out to me about working together. I looked at my dashboard where I tracked the number of approved and potential hours and was able to let this prospect know I could begin working on their project in four to five weeks. Without this tracking, I would not have been able to provide this accurate timeline for my future client.

The number of approved hours is my most important indicator for dictating my activity for today. The number of potential hours becomes my most important indicator to determine what I need to do to get new business and earn more money.

A Word Of Caution

In the early years at Noodlehead Marketing, I was chronically bad about counting my eggs before they hatched. In fact, I'd communicate this idealism I had towards projects coming to fruition with my team and vendors.

Unfortunately, this unfounded optimism led to chronic disappointment. It also led to a stagnation in sales activity because we expected the potential work to finalize so we pulled back on our efforts. After numerous issues resulting from this approach, I shifted my expectations to the place that a deal was not done until the commitment was made and money was exchanged.

The benefit of this approach was that if the deal actually came through, there were also others right behind it because we kept on doing what we needed to grow the business. As a result of my experiences, my recommendation is not to plan around potential work. Instead plan around actual paid projects.

Red Zone: 10 Actions To Increase Income

In red alert mode, we need to move quickly to get paying gigs. Ideally, we've discovered what to do in red alert mode before it happens as I've described previously. For those of you who are in this zone now, here are ten actions to help you quickly move forward and suppress the panic.

1. Since God knows and is in control, anchor yourself by praying for direction. Don't believe God is there? Talk to a mentor or someone you look up to for help in getting grounded.
2. Meet with ten to twelve people per week, ranging from good friends to people you hardly know and ask for advice.
3. Call past clients and leads to discover if they have any needs you can help with.
4. Reach out to people who've referred work your way in the past and let them know your situation and how they can help.
5. Keep your inner circle updated on your situation and how they can help you overcome it. Be specific with what you need.
6. Attend two to three networking events per week where you can meet numerous people in a short period.
7. Get exposed on-line by sharing articles, content and ideas on Facebook, Linkedin, and Twitter.

8. Blog daily and share links to your blogs with your network. If you don't have a site, signup for a free account on Linkedin, Medium or Wordpress.
9. Offer to write a blog for those in your network who have platforms and an audience.
10. Slow the bleeding by taking odd jobs, research study groups, or becoming an extra in a feature film.

While there are specific actions we can do to take responsibility and move forward in our lives, it's hard to do it on our own, and this is why we'll want a strong community around us. Let's explore what it looks like to build an emotional support system.

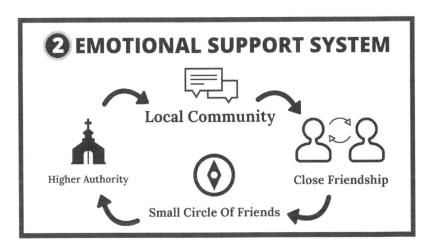

Checkpoint 2 - Emotional Support System

There is a distinct difference between running a company and freelancing, and it wasn't until I shut down our business did I recognize it. When we face difficulties and trouble leading a group, there is a sense the team could work together to overcome any obstacle we were facing. In my experience running a business, I did not feel alone or solely responsible for the success and failure of our endeavors since others were around to help. When we had success, there were others to celebrate and realize the meaning behind these moments.

When I stepped into the world of freelancing, I felt naked in this regard. Everything hung on me, and there was no team to help me up or hide behind when things got bad. Entering into freelancing, I now felt a new sense of vulnerability.

It was now time to step out and stand up. One way to empower me to do so was establishing an emotional support system because even on our own as freelancers, we need support, encouragement and guidance from others.

With numerous ways to create and sustain an emotional support system, I've identified four ideas to help start the process of building one that works best for you. Let's dig into the first.

Anchor Into A Higher Authority

Going down an unknown road raises questions, concerns, and problems. Many of which, we won't know how to answer, address or face. We'll likely need someone or something outside ourselves we can anchor into during these potentially stressful moments and seasons.

A higher authority is a powerful emotional anchor because we're tapping into help from someone who has gone before us and can provide insights we ourself cannot see or understand. When we're struggling and emotionally distraught, this insight will become more valuable than we expected before starting the journey.

For me, I've decided to anchor into the highest authority, God. Reading through the history, letters and biographies (Bible) of people on the front lines of God's story provides me with insights, guidance, and direction for what I face in my personal and professional life. This advice is timeless and the more I read it, the more applicable it becomes to the challenges I face.

If you lack or reject a belief in God, consider anchoring into a mentorship, someone you look up to, or a parent that you respect and love. We're looking for someone who has gone before us, reflected on their journey and has powerful and meaningful insights to help guide us when the fog is thick.

In searching for and selecting a mentor, carefully examine their life and example. When I first moved from Arizona to Atlanta, I did not know what I was doing and needed help. Unfortunately, several unhealthy individuals sought me out to mentor me. They were toxic people who did not live their lives in a way that modeled a positive and fruitful example. While I learned a great deal during these times, it resulted in many wounds and pain that affect me to this day.

There are great leaders, and there are toxic leaders. Take the time to find a healthy mentor who models attributes you aspire to mimic.

Lean Into A Close Friendship

Having a close friend is important to flourish as a freelancer. For this role, we can consider a significant other, close family member, or a critical friend. We want someone who laments the lows with us and helps us walk through tough times towards better future outcomes.

Finding a friend who is going down the same road of freelancing is empowering as it provides unique and dynamic interactions. It also fosters a context to develop a deep friendship from our shared experiences.

A year into my freelancing journey, there was a friend who posted a nice doodle of a sermon by Andy Stanley. I liked the post on Twitter and followed him. Shortly after, we began messaging back and forth. Both located in the Atlanta area, we decided to get together. While meeting, we connected on many levels and he disclosed he was about to enter the freelancing world. We turned out to be a perfect match for a new friendship.

In our close and serendipitous connection, we found it valuable to help each other towards our respective destinations as freelancers. It would have been much harder to have traversed this road without this friend.

Cultivate A Small Circle Of Friends

Looking up to a higher authority and having a close friendship are critical to building our wall of sandbags to hold back the emotional flood waters of freelancing.

What we also need is a small circle of friends we can honestly open up to and share what we're facing. They also act as a collection of wise counselors giving insights, ideas, connections, and resources. We want friends that will elevate us during tough times and celebrate our wins along the way.

Before I launched into freelancing, I spent three months meeting with about a dozen people per week. I had also started frequently attending a Bible study of mostly older business men.

When I hit the ground running as a freelancer, there were people from my network that I assembled into my small circle of friends. In my entire freelancing journey, I've always had a sense of reassurance that there was a group of people I could go to when I needed it.

At the same time as my transition, I also witnessed a friend lose his job, and he did not have a small circle of friends in his life. Sadly, he struggled mightily since he was on his own with almost no one to help. Watching him gave me a deep sense of gratitude realizing what I had.

Build Local Community

Since we certainly can't go on this journey alone, and it's a bit much to ask just a few people to help carry our burden when we need it, an extended community provides encouragement, meals, child care, help around the house, and moving. When we're wearing the heavy burden of freelancing, every bit of help and support we can get is huge to our long-term sustainability.

When we transitioned from our marketing company to freelancing, we had a strong intimate community through our local church. It was a place and group of people we could get rest and support along the journey. I had other community through past clients, people who worked with and for me, and people I had helped when I was in positions to do so.

A local community in place is reassuring and helpful in so many little ways, but it's hard to appreciate unless we've experienced them rallying behind us.

With emotional support in place, we also want to have a financial buffer to help carry us through the times of famine. The water tower is a powerful tool to help us do this.

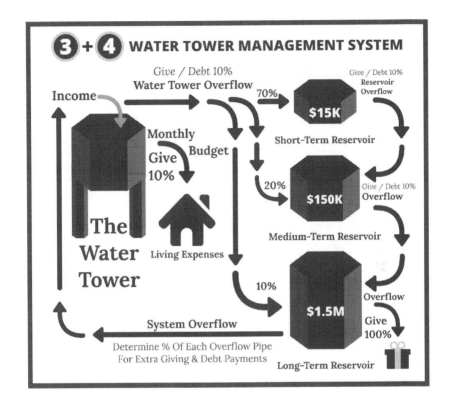

Checkpoint 3 - The Water Tower

With a red, yellow, green system in place, we'll know what to do when we're under stress and panicking. This is powerful. Having an emotional support system in place to help work through the emotions of the experience is important.

What we also need is a financial buffer to empower us to fulfill our financial responsibilities when things are going well and when they are not.

To start, we've got to determine our baseline. Our baseline is the amount of money that indicates we've hit rock bottom financially. This visibility gives us a reference point to leverage.

When it comes to determining our baseline, It comes down to three options. Zero dollars, some amount below zero dollars (debt) or some amount above zero dollars (savings).

For some, a baseline might be ten thousand dollars on their credit card. For others, it might be when they have no cash left in their bank account. For those of us who want to flourish in freelancing, we'll choose to make our baseline a strategic amount of money we have in reserve.

This cash flow reserve is our water tower, and the water tower is how we fund our living expenses and future savings.

The way I personally tally the amount of the water tower is by adding up the money in the business checking account, personal checking account and the amount owed to me by clients in accounts receivables (unpaid invoices). From there, I subtract any money we have on our credit card, and this gives me my total water tower amount.

To determine the amount of money I wanted my water tower to hold required I take a look at my monthly income. At the time of my water towers inception, we paid ourselves slightly over five thousand dollars per month. Having a three month supply of cash seemed like an appropriate amount for the water tower, so I decided to make it fifteen thousand dollars.

This amount also meant that clients could pay us late, we could go over budget and we'd be able to pay unexpected expenses without going into debt. Moreover, this financial buffer would help prevent the stress that comes with financial troubles.

Stuff happens in life, but instead of stopping at that realization let's live in a way that expects it. This way we're covered when the dips happen and if they don't come, we get ahead faster.

Once I came up with the water tower concept and set our goal for fifteen thousand dollars, it took us a year to fill it up. Along the way, it helped us through some slow and personally challenging seasons. A few months after we filled it, we were hit with a perfect storm of circumstances that could have been brutal to withstand without the water tower in place.

It was at the beginning of 2016, and I had two clients who had committed to work with me for twenty hours per month. At the same time, both had to pause their engagement with me. This change meant three thousand dollars I was expecting to earn was not going to come in. On top of this, I had two clients that owed me another three thousand dollars that both had to pay me late. This resulted in a six thousand dollar shortfall.

Thanks to a full water tower, we were able to weather the wait on getting paid late without struggling to meet personal financial obligations. The expected work deficit ended up getting met by a client increasing his hours and some new customers working with me.

In another season, there was a client I was working for that went out of business. As a result, I did not get paid two thousand dollars I was owed. This shortfall was an important and painful loss, but in light of our full water tower, it didn't affect our lives in any significant way.

If we had not had the water tower when these storms hit, it would have been stressful for my family and me to figure out how we'd weather the difficulty.

Expecting & preparing for these storms allows us to minimize their impact when they come. The Water Tower is one way to do it, but to truly insulate ourselves; we'll need to take the Water Tower one step further.

Checkpoint 4 - Water Tower Management System

With a full water tower in place, the organic next step is to determine where we put the surplus income when the tower overflows. As part of this, we also want to determine how we'll address short, medium and long-term financial goals. And, how we set up the system to facilitate debt repayment and giving is important.

To set up our water tower management system, we need to determine how much we want to save in the short, medium and long term. We also will want to determine how much we want to give once we've reached our goals and how much we want to give along the way. We also need to determine our stance when it comes to debt and how we'll pay it back, should we have or accrue it.

The Three Reservoirs

Let's start with our short-term savings. Imagine having a fund that would allow us to buy the smaller things we need or want. The laptop is old, and we need a new one. The couch is worn out and stained by raising kids. How great would it be to simply get a new notebook computer and a replacement sofa? This is the idea of the short-term savings.

To keep it simple, I decided to make our short-term savings the same as our water tower, fifteen thousand dollars. In my mind, this amount of money would cover any expenses that may pop-up either by need or preference.

For medium-term savings, I think of buying a car or a house. To keep it simple and also make our number relevant, I simply added a zero to my short-term savings amount and determined our medium-term savings to be $150k. When this reservoir is full, this will allow us to either pay cash for a house or a significant down payment.

Now, when it came to discovering my long-term savings, I wanted to have an amount that would generate enough interest to fund our annual income. Before taxes, I figured $75k per year would be a good amount to shoot for. $1.5M would be the target to fund this at a conservative return rate of five percent. This is our long-term savings target. As part of this calculation, we'll also want to consider the rate of inflation.

To summarize, we determined the following three as our savings goals.

Short-Term Reservoir	Medium-Term Reservoir	Long-Term Reservoir
$15,000	$150,000	$1.5 Million

While this acts as a great example and reference point for you, each of us has a different context so determine what goals work best for you. The beauty of defining these financial goals, the win, is it allows us to determine what it takes to make progress towards them.

With purposeful money, we prevent falling into the trap of always wanting more and never being content with what we have. Instead, we'll have the direction to move towards accomplishing our goals.

Where Giving & Debt Fit In This Process

With our financial structure in place, let's dive down into our strategy for debt repayment and giving, starting with the latter.

Let's Talk About Giving

To get us going, let me share a quote from Paul the Apostle.

[9]"Remember this—a farmer who plants only a few seeds will get a small crop. But the one who plants generously will get a generous crop. **You must each decide in your heart how much to give. And don't give reluctantly or in response to pressure.** "For God loves a person who gives cheerfully." And God will generously provide all you need. Then you will always have everything you need and plenty left over to share with others."

As a Christian, I believe we are called to give generously and this snippet, from the Apostle Paul's letter to a group of Christians in Corinth, gives us direction on how to go about this. Whether we're a Christian or not, it's best for us to decide beforehand how much we want to joyfully give.

We've made our family's goal to give away one hundred percent of our surplus. This commitment means that once the water tower and three reservoirs are full, we would give all additional income away. Once our present and future needs are taken care of, there is no personal desire for my wife and me to accumulate wealth.

Saving this amount of income will take years, so to facilitate giving beforehand, we've established a giving process as we progress towards this. To start, we give ten percent of the budget we pay ourselves monthly.

We then give ten percent in each step where there is an overflow. When the water tower overflows into the short-term savings reservoir, we give ten percent of it away.

---

[9] Paul The Apostle, 2 Corinthians 9:6-8

When the short term reservoir fills up, it overflows into the medium term reservoir. We give ten percent of it away. The same goes for when the medium-term overflows into the long-term savings. When the long-term reservoir is filled up, all of the overflow would be given away.

The closer we get to accomplishing our goals, the more we give. But, before we can give generously, we need to resolve our debt situation.

Debt

When it comes to giving our money away, we can give it to those who need it, or we can give it away to banks for lending us their money. I'm pretty sure we'd all like to avoid giving it to the banks, but unfortunately, that does not tend to be our cultural reality.

My wife and I accumulated over $140k in student loans, including interest, and will pay it off around 2019. We pay about eleven-hundred dollars per month towards this debt. To help accelerate paying off the loan, we took the surplus income, outlined above, from the giving section to make extra debt payments. Simply put, we hijacked some of our extra giving to pay off our student loans. At first, we did half and half towards giving and debt repayment acceleration. We then decided to move all of it towards debt repayment acceleration.

And then, we decided it was time to buy a house, so we shifted gears. To accelerate saving a down payment, we leveraged this surplus. Once we saved the down payment, we shifted the surplus towards paying off our student loans.

Once those are paid off, we'll change the surplus back to extra giving.

Wrapping Up Our Fifth Achievement

There will be ups and downs financially, emotionally and physically in our journey. Setting up systems and structures to prevent the adverse effects in our personal and professional lives will relieve the level of stress and anxiety we feel. When we can't prevent the down times, our goal is to minimize how they negatively affect us.

When we can't minimize their effect, we've got a safety net in God and community to help us out of any hole we find ourselves in. We've also got a set of actions we can move on to make our situation better.

To review, here are the four checkpoints that help stabilize us.

1. Active Color Zone System
2. Emotional Support System
3. Water Tower
4. Water Tower System

Any of us who have ridden the roller coaster of freelancing find great joy when we arrive at a place where it no longer affects us. It almost seems like we become a different and better person. It's here we can enjoy our work and time off.

We realize our work is not a prison but is instead a place where we can enjoy, learn and grow. It gives us the margin to spend more time organizing and directing our money in a way that aligns with our objectives.

Vital Achievement #6 Wise and Precise Financial Management

I once heard it said, we can either be controlled by our money or we can control money for our intended purposes. When you look at how you manage money, which better describes you?

I've had seasons in the business and freelancing where everything is perfectly and proactively managed well. I've had others times where years of unorganized financial activity has accumulated. Quite honestly, this topic and task can be quite boring and tedious. It's something all of us can quickly discard as not important. Unfortunately, it seems when we're not willing and able to manage this well, we'll fail quickly and easily.

So as a freelancer, it's vital we keep our financial management as simple and easy as possible. Doing so allows us to focus on what we do the best while also not getting bogged down by the baggage of complex structure.

Success in this achievement provides us the visibility to respond in situations wisely. The first step in the process is us getting legit as a freelancer.

① LEGIT BUSINESS & BANK ACCOUNTS

Establish Business Entity

Explore The Option's Pros & Cons

- Sole Proprietorship
- "S" Corporation (S Corp)
- Limited Liability Corporation (LLC)

Setup Business Financial Accounts
Checking + Savings
Credit Card Processing

Checkpoint 1 - Legit Business And Bank Accounts

It's not uncommon to start freelancing without a legal business entity or setting up bank accounts. While this may be the easier road, I've found it more than worth it to set up a business entity and establish separate financial bank accounts once we're fully committed to the vocation.

In 2009, our marketing company was audited by the IRS for our 2008 taxes. The business was set up, but it was setup as a sole proprietorship, not a corporation. In this case, the IRS did not see any differentiation between the business and our personal lives. This gray zone made it tough to reconcile the challenges coming from this tax audit and allowed them to explain many of our claimed expenses as personal ones even when they were not.

While not all of us will face an IRS audit, it's sloppy management not to get legit as a freelancer. It also makes it harder to precisely see what is going on and how to address different issues that arise along the way.

When I started freelancing, I used our prior marketing business' entity and bank accounts for my freelancing funds. Since I was not sure that freelancing would become my main vocation, I chose this easier road.

Eighteen months in, I had dealt with an issue related to the past business' merchant services and had the need for establishing business insurance to work with one of my new clients. By this time, I was also fully committed to freelancing, so it was appropriate to start a new business entity. I started a new S corporation with the name Protheseos, which means intentional in Greek.

Starting an S corporation gave the option to pay me a dividend on a payroll, and this option saves money on taxes. Generating a substantial income, I benefitted from this structure. If you're starting out, you may not profit from an S corp and could do just as well with a simple LLC. Consult a CPA to figure out what is best in your situation.

As part of the process of establishing the company, I wanted to make my wife, and I equal partners. This was a way of communicating our mutual commitment to this career path. If you're married or about to be, I'd highly recommend discussing this option with your significant other.

With this new company created, my next step included setting up checking and savings bank accounts for the company. While most banks will work well, I found Chase was the best fit for me. One of the reasons was the ability to deposit checks using their app on my iPhone. This digital channel eliminated ninety percent of my bank visits.

In addition to the bank accounts, you'll likely also need a credit card processor to take payment from certain clients. After some research, I found Stripe a great option. It is quick and easy to setup, takes all forms of credit cards and integrates with numerous online services.

Now that I've mentioned credit card processing, you may be wondering if you should sign up for a credit card. I'd recommend steering away from using credit cards. While they can be useful, they also are easy for us to rack up a large debt quickly. Credit cards have the ability to create a false sense of safety that can prevent us from quickly taking care of the issues we need to address.

At Noodlehead Marketing, I set up a business credit card. We did well using it and paying it off every month to get the bonuses. As time went on, we hired a sales team member who was paid partially on a salary. After three months, we used up our financial reserves paying his salary and could no longer afford to pay him.

I was so emotionally and financially invested in this person; I did not want to let him go. I thought if we gave him more time, he'd pull it together and generate the income needed to make his salary sustainable. Since I had the credit card, I could buy us more time. Unfortunately, three months later and fifteen thousand dollars on the credit card, we didn't succeed, and I had to let him go. I was left to deal with the debt. If I had not had the credit card, it would have forced me to deal with the issue at hand instead of kicking the can down the road three months later.

On the flipside, my wife and I used a credit card when I first started my freelancing work as a way to manage the cash flow inconsistencies and issues.

Unfortunately, it masked some of the issues we were facing and delayed us creating the responsive budget, which we'll discuss in the seventh achievement. We had also not yet established a water tower cash flow and so the credit card acted as our water tower fund. It was a tool we needed to bridge the gap, but it was one I worked quickly to move away from. It's unpleasant to be dependent on debt to live.

When it comes down to it, getting a credit card is a decision you'll have to make for yourself. When you make the decision consider the risk that comes with it.

Checkpoint 2 - We're Easily Watching What We Track

With our bank accounts set up and our debit cards in our wallet, we can start sending and receiving money. With these transactions, we'll want to make sure we track and categorize these activities.

When I transitioned into Freelancing, I needed to seek out a new financial management system. In my search, I explored Freshbooks, Xero, and Less Accounting. After digging in deeper, I decided to go with the freelancer-friendly and simple accounting tool LessAccounting.

It tracks bank account transactions, sends invoices, integrates with Stripe Payments and has a variety of reports. It had everything I wanted and was simple to use. My wife and I received a weekly email report of the week's financial activity. After testing this tool out, I also had a pleasant and responsive experience with their customer support.

I'd encourage you to explore these services, others you find on your own, and tools recommended to you by friends. Pick the tool which helps you best accomplish your goals.

Invoices

Tracking who owes us money and when that money is due is critical to financial sustainability. We can get so caught up in work; we don't know who owes us money and how much is due.

Weekly, I'm looking at the total amount of money owed to me and which invoices are late. When the invoice hits its due date, I'm sending a friendly email to the client checking in on payment and discovering when I can expect to receive it.

When it comes to financial struggles, I've had more issues with cash flow than I have with the volume of work. Keep an eye on those invoices and make sure the checks are coming in.

Time Tracking

Since I'm billing for my time using BAM (Batch Action Management), I need time tracking. Initially, I used a spreadsheet to track how much time I was working with each client. While this can be a great starting point, it is limiting and more time intensive than other options. As a result, I explored several time tracking tools and found the freelancer-friendly Timecamp to be the best tool for what I needed. They've got a good computer and iPhone widget that easily allows me to tag the project I'm working on and log the time. I easily switch projects and run reports to see how many hours I've logged for the day, week, month and year, collectively and by the client.

For each client I have in Timecamp, I also add the number of hours I billed. This allows me to know quickly when I'm about to complete a batch or when I'm billing reactively; it allows me to see how many hours I've logged since they last paid. Both of these insights act as triggers for sending invoices and throttling my time.

A Final Note On Watching What We Track

While watching our money is helpful, focusing too much on it can be dangerous. We can't change the number by looking at it. Let's instead focus on the work in front of us and in the pipeline. We can then take the actions we need to generate income. Simply put, focus on the cause of the growing income, not the growing income itself. Otherwise, when we find ourself in panic mode, it'll be too late to figure out how we recover.

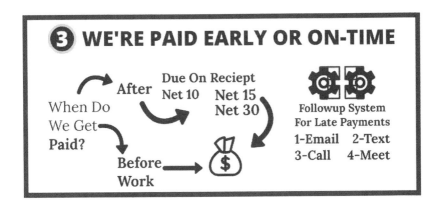

Checkpoint 3 - We're Paid On-Time

As freelancers, managing cash flow is critical to minimizing our stress and equipping ourselves to fulfill our financial obligations.

When I started freelancing, I invoiced clients in batches of ten hours at the start of the batch with payment due in fifteen days. For the most part, customers paid early or on time but when they didn't I sent an email reminder.

When the due date passes, I'll send an email asking what their plan is for payment on the invoice. As their tardiness increases, my communication frequency and mediums increase as well. In many cases, I'll get updates from clients when they're late, but sometimes I've got to text, call or on rare occasions, show up in person to get paid.

To help minimize the time receiving payment I changed my payment terms from fifteen to ten days. Since I started freelancing, my goal has been to make it as easy as possible for clients to work with me and so I balance terms with the realistic accounting practices of my clients.

If I wanted to ensure I got paid early, I'd require payment before starting work. The more demand I create as a freelancer, the more leverage I'll have to demand better payment terms.

Currently, I operate with net ten and will apply stricter terms for those who pay late and require me chasing them down to get paid.

I'll push clients who chronically pay recurring invoices late to switch to quarterly, semi-annual or annual payment terms. This restructure results in less invoices to send out, fewer payments for them to send my way and less reminders for late payments.

If there is an issue with invoicing or payments, find a way to make it easier for the client to pay and a win for us.

Mitigating The Risk Of Not Getting Paid

Whether we're running a business or working as a freelancer, there will be times when we don't get paid. While there were a few small instances early on, it wasn't until two years in did I face this problem at a significant level. In fact, there were three cases where this issue arose in 2016.

I got reconnected with an old business colleague who hired me to help him with his investor presentation. We worked for almost twenty hours on his project narrowing down his book of information into a handful of meaningful and compelling slides. When we concluded the project, he was ecstatic about the work I had done to the point it made him tear up.

Unfortunately, he did not have the funds to pay the invoice and instead was relying on the investment dollars he was expecting to receive shortly. Fourteen months later, it never arrived, and I did not get the two thousand dollars. Thankfully, he was very open about the situation and stayed in contact along the way. He did offer to pay me more than he originally agreed, to make up for the delay, but unfortunately, he never received funds to pay me.

It would have been nice to know ahead of time about the risk I was taking so I could have made the decision to do the work with that understanding. Thankfully, when I did the work, it was a light month and it did not cause me to turn down other work that would have paid me.

The second scenario happened several months later when I was referred to a new customer. The work we were doing was going quite well until he decided to move forward on a project that was beyond what he could fund. I sensed this due to his late payments on the invoices. While this was stressful, he did always pay the invoice, even if they were late.

There were a few points where he requested I continue the project with the invoices outstanding. At those points, I knew I should have shifted to require payment up-front instead of ten days after invoicing. In my attempt to satisfy him and minimize the risk of not getting paid, I continued working on the project accruing a debt of a thousand dollars. After following up by email, phone, and text his responses became more sporadic until he ignored me altogether. I reached out to an employee and informal business partner to help move it along with no progress. Unlike the first, he cut off communication making it stressful. I finally decided to let it go and trust God would resolve it on my behalf. I had to move on and did not want this bogging me down.

The third situation was one I went into knowing it was risky, but I knew I could help the owner. The company was struggling in its recent pivot to right the ship after neglect and a recent mutiny. I ended up tallying seventy-five hours. The first fifty hours were paid on time or early so things looked good to start. Unfortunately, the problems were so severe in this company there was little I could do to help turn it around.

If it was the Titanic, my role was not to stop the ship from sinking but rather to offer a lifeboat to the people caught in it's destruction. As I saw this trajectory become more apparent, I had hit the fifty-hour mark. It was at this point I had the instinct to stop working on this project because I may not get paid for the additional time logged.

Unfortunately, I got caught in the tide of wanting to help and ended up getting financially hurt in the end. It was another two thousand dollars I was not going to receive.

While these were expensive lessons to learn, I'm grateful to have learned them during the most successful year of freelancing I've had, and in the context of an active water tower management system. Sustaining these achievements allowed me to let the money go quicker and easier while also prioritizing the relationships above the dollars. Holding onto money and grudges is an excellent way to self-destruct. As much as it hurts, it's better to move forward and adjust our boundaries to prevent similar situations from playing out poorly.

A Quick Rule To Prevent Over Reliance

While there may be temporary exceptions, we want to generally make sure no client pays us more than thirty percent of our monthly income. By allowing a client to pay us more, we increase our risk and lose our leverage to push back when appropriate. Should the client go out of business or fire us, the consequence is much more severe the more we rely on the income of any one customer.

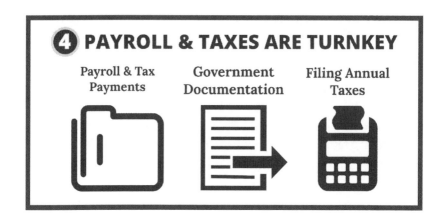

Checkpoint 4 - Payroll & Taxes Turnkey

I inherited the secret of making payroll and taxes easy from growing and managing a team at Noodlehead Marketing. After a few bad payroll experiences, we came across an outsourced HR & payroll company. They handled the paperwork, payroll, taxes and company quarterly taxes all in one place for a reasonable fee. It was great, and it made it easier to run the business knowing we had a partner helping alleviate some of the infrastructure needs.

When I transitioned into freelancing, I continued to use their services running payroll. Their service made it easier to pay me, track income and manage taxes.

At the end of each year, they provide me with W2 forms that I pass to my CPA for filing. When we keep our accounting transactions up to date and manage our income through a payroll service, we can quickly and easily file our taxes.

In the business, there were years where I was filing taxes late and had to file extensions which delayed our tax filing from the spring to the fall. Since we usually got a refund, this only delayed us getting the money back.

As I grew as an individual and we learned from some poor management, we got our act together, and in the last several years of Noodlehead Marketing, we got our taxes done on-time or early. When I transitioned to freelancing, I continued this habit of filing business and personal taxes returns by the end of February. Filing early allows us to receive our refund quicker or, if we owe money, it gives us a window of time to save.

Anything we can do to make our lives easier and more focused on the work is going to maximize our ability to achieve our larger goals. While there are some fees associated with outsourcing payroll, I've found the benefit outweighs the cost.

An alternative option to using a payroll company is hiring a solid CPA. They can help handle the quarterly and annual tax filings in addition to guiding you through the minefield of potential money and tax issues. When it comes to payroll and taxes, find someone you trust to lead the way.

Wrapping Up The Sixth Achievement

Ultimately, we want to manage our time; the money owed to us and the money we spend so we can make wise decisions to help us more efficiently reach our goals.

To review, here are the four checkpoints we'll hit along the way towards precise and wise financial management.

1. Legit Business & Bank Accounts
2. We're Easily Watching What We Track
3. We're Paid On-Time
4. Payroll & Taxes Are Turnkey

With financial visibility, it's still hard to see problems and react accordingly. Without it, it's impossible. While it may seem boring, this achievement can be the difference between surviving and thriving.

Which will you choose?

Vital Achievement #7 Unified Personal & Work Lives

Our personal intentions are projected through our work, and our business affects our personal lives. Manage this tension well, and we maximize the benefits. Handle it poorly, and our life spirals into a state of isolation and chaos.

After my wife and I moved to Atlanta in 2005, I slowly became consumed with work. Two years into launching our business I was working every day and all the time. The very values of faith and marriage that I cared for were the very things I neglected in the pursuit of my desires. With fragmented relationships all around me, unity became a distant thought.

In this achievement, we'll explore how we prevent this fragmentation from permeating our lives and what we can do to cultivate unity when it seems beyond our grasp. Let's get to it!

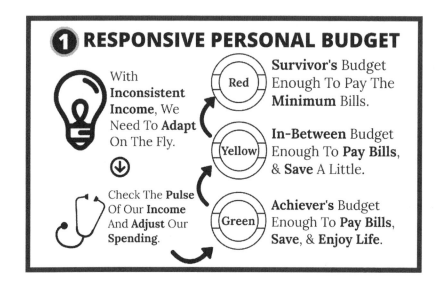

Checkpoint 1 - Responsive Personal Budget

I started freelancing with an abundance of paid work. Within a few months I had eight projects from others reaching out as a result of relational seeds planted years before.

While this was an unexpected success, it created a problem I was not expecting. We were making money, but we did not have anything to show for it. Why was there a balance on our credit card and no money left in our accounts when we made more money than we needed?

As I investigated, I realized we were not spending in accordance with our fluctuating income. We instead spent like we were receiving a consistent salary.

If this trend had continued, we would not only have limited or progress but also regressed into debt. So, I leveraged the red, yellow, green system I was using and created a responsive personal budget we would follow.

This new budget created the visibility and accountability to cut back our spending when our income was not there to support it. As part of the responsive system, we established three budget scenarios.

The first was our red survivor's budget. How little could we spend and still take care of our main responsibilities? What services could we downgrade or pause based on a red level month? What expenses, like eating out and driving, could we cut out or back to decrease our costs?

As I answered these questions, I created a budget just over $3,000. This budget was our barebones survival zone. On the flip-side, I wanted to determine our green zone which would consist of a budget that covers our expenses, allows some freedom to spend, and contributes towards savings and giving. At the conclusion of this discovery, we determined our budget to be $5,150 per month after taxes. This was our achiever's budget.

With the top and bottom tiers established, the yellow zone was an amount between the two numbers. With the zone boundaries defined we could now easily determine our spending.

At the end of each month, I reviewed our finances and how much income we had from paid freelancing work. Depending on how much money was available to pay ourselves determined our budget for the subsequent month.

A green month in my freelancing work led to a green month in personal spending. The same went for yellow and red.

This was the catalyst that led to the creation of the water tower system. Having a reserve of cash eventually eliminated the need for a responsive budget because we were buffered from the ups and down of our freelancing income. Until we had that reserve, the responsive budget was critical.

If we face unexpected circumstances or droughts in our future, we may have to pull the responsive budget back out. It serves a purpose for a short time but after reaching certain goals, it is no longer needed on a regular basis.

Figure out what your personal zones are and create your responsive budget to adapt to the circumstances of freelancing.

2 WE BRING FAMILY (OR CLOSE FRIENDS) ALONG

Whether It's Our Spouse, Parents, Or Kids, We'll **Bring Those Affected** By Our Freelancing **Along**.

Share Freelancing **Wins & Losses**.

Communicate The **Progression** & **Regression**.

Checkpoint 2 - We Bring Family *(Or Close Friends)* Along

For those of us who are married, have family members and friends reliant on our provision, It's important we bring them into the fold when it comes to the status of our freelancing activities.

We want to ensure we're on the same page and we also want to provide reassurance to our loved ones that we're doing the things we need to be doing to move forward in our lives.

I've done the opposite, and it can cause a lot of trouble in a marriage or friendship. In regards to the story I shared earlier about accruing fifteen thousand dollars in debt, I didn't tell my wife until it was too late. She said if she had known, she would have altered her spending habits to make it easier on us. By not communicating, it made the entire situation worse.

For a moment, pretend you've got a teenager at home. I know, scary huh? Now let's say you tell the teenager they need to take care of their chores this week. They respond with sure, I'll take care of it.

Their response evokes little to no confidence in their ability and commitment to take care of their chores. Especially if they lack any history to prove otherwise.

Now, let's imagine the same scenario plays out but they instead respond that they'll clean their room, put the dishes away and take out the garbage by tomorrow morning. Once they're done, they will check in to make sure it was all completed as expected.

The second approach is reassuring. It provides confidence it will get done and specifics of when it'll be complete. We want to apply this same practice when communicating with our spouse or family.

Part of the problem we faced with our inconsistent income was not having the cash on hand to pay for the things we were buying. We lacked visibility. Once I realized this, I created the visibility, but I had to communicate it with my wife so we could both curtail our spending accordingly.

This communication morphed into an end-of-month communication update that included our budget for the upcoming month, the number of hours I worked, how much we had in our water tower and what our savings reservoirs looked like. While my wife is not my boss, she is my partner, and I want us both to see the information that is relevant to our decision making.

Since I was already tracking this information for myself, it was only a few extra steps to communicate it with my wife. I also found communicating this eliminated some of the tension on her purchases I was pushing back on. Now we both had the same insight and she could make decisions for herself on what and when we shopped.

It's important to focus on sharing insights that are most relevant to those we are sharing them with. We want to prevent overwhelming or desensitizing them. We can easily find ourselves tracking many factors that are helpful, but we need to filter it down to the most relevant and valuable insights when sharing.

For Different Reasons, We Need Structure

Early in our marriage, I was a free spirit. Think of a kite flying around in the sky and that was me. Unfortunately, I was so busy floating among the clouds I lost track of reality and the responsibilities around me.

My wife was a structured high achiever. She stayed grounded because she was the product of past kite-flying people. She was the one who dealt with the consequences of their actions.

To leverage a metaphor, I imagine us both as bouncy balls. I was bouncing everywhere I possibly could with no limits. She was a bouncy ball not moving at all. We both needed a box, to bounce in. For me, I needed a box so I could bounce around freely, but not get out of hand. She needed a box so she could feel free to bounce around.

With the structure in place, we both bounced around freely, but how the structure helped us each was different. Structure gave me freedom to move and provide enough constraint that my actions did not harm people, and instead uplifted and empowered them. Structure gave my wife the boundaries where she could move freely, and it allowed her to act when she otherwise would have felt paralyzed to do so.

We're going to have people in our lives that are different than us and it's important we bring others along in a way that empowers us and reassures them. Structure is one way to do this and the eight achievements in this book are the framework to help you do this.

Examples Of Bringing Others Along

In 2016, we committed to buying a house. As a result, we had to save more than we had for our down payment and cash reserves. We also wanted to accelerate the process so we chose to throw every dollar we could at it.

In reflection of the earlier part of the year, we also realized we could save a good amount of money by strictly following our budget. Doing so also meant little to no eating out and no going to the movie theaters.

Right after we made these decisions, I had a friend invite me to see a film with him in a group setting. I told him I was unable to go to the film. Privately, I communicated to him why I was unable to go. He immediately volunteered to pay for my movie. A few weeks later, another friend reached out to invite me to a meal and movie. I declined and told him the reason. He too volunteered to pay for both.

You probably get where I'm going with this. When we're open, and we share with those who care about us, it gives them an opportunity to fill the gap when we can't. When we don't disclose, we potentially rob them of the opportunity.

I enjoy computer games, and there are several times when I've bought a friend a game I wanted to play it with so they didn't have to overcome the obstacle of purchasing it. Most of us care more about the relationship, so when we're able to, we are more than willing to cover the cost of others. Bring our family and close friends along and allow them to be a part of our journey by helping to carry the load. Let go of your pride and embrace the support.

While it may feel easier to share with others when we're on a budget, it's also important to share when we are going through rough financial times. It can be fruitful to disclose the situation to our spouse, children, and close friends in an appropriate way. No one can help or encourage if they don't know what is going on.

3 ACTIVE RHYTHMS OF REST & RELEASE

Take **Daily, Weekly, Monthly,** & **Annual Breaks** From Work.

Take Time To **Ramp Up** Our Activites And **Close Down** Our work.

Checkpoint 3 - Active Rhythms Of Rest & Release

Running a marathon is no easy task, and as a freelancer, that's what we're doing. For long term success, we'll want to recognize our limitations and embrace them.

I've held onto strict boundaries for work and rest. As my journey has progressed, my boundaries and rest rhythm have evolved for the better. While I'm quite effective at managing this tension now, it was not always like this.

Growing up, I was taught to take a day of the week to rest, release and show reverence to God. For Christians, we call this the Sabbath. It's so important; it was one of the ten commandments to Moses.

"Remember to observe the Sabbath day by keeping it holy."[10]

The first several years in Atlanta, I adhered to this command. As our marketing company grew, I began taking more control of my destiny and trusting God less. When things got worse, I worked more. This workload was also a

---

[10] Exodus 20:8 NLT

way for me to escape the things in my life I did not want to face.

Unfortunately, when business would get better, I did not cut back my workload so the amount of time I worked grew over time. One Sunday turned to two Sundays, turned to every Sunday. Before I knew it, I was working every day and all the time. This road led to chaos, burn out and an overall sad existence.

I recently visited a former employee of our marketing company, and she recalled how far and fast I would go only to crash and burn for weeks at a time. It was a good reminder of how intense I could go at it.

During these stressful seasons, any outsider could see my way of doing things was not working. I was repeating the cycle getting to the point where I could not take it anymore. At my breaking point, I prayed that God would show me a better way.

Shortly after this prayer, a friend reminded me of the Sabbath, and he asked if I was taking one.

NO, I was not.

At that point, I had realized how it had slowly been phased out of my life. I decided to take back this day of rest and began down a road of working less and trusting God to do more. While working less seemed backward, life got better, and I became more productive working fewer hours. Finally, I was able to start enjoying life again.

Whether you believe in God, don't know or don't care we all need to acknowledge our need for rest and release, so let's take a look at the subject from another point of view.

A Practical Way To Look At Pacing Ourselves

We can also make a case for rest by looking at some grounded research on the topic.

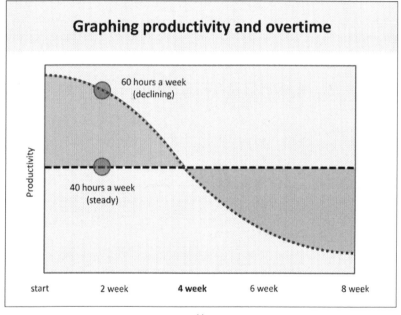

11

In the diagram above, Daniel Cook shares a powerful visual that communicates how pacing ourselves affects our productivity.

11 Rules Of Productivity by Daniel Cook - http://www.lostgarden.com/2008/09/rules-of-productivity-presentation.html

By working a regular week of forty hours, we are more productive over time. If we increase our volume of work, we find a surplus of productivity, but we also get a steep decline over time. I equate this to credit cards. When we use credit cards, we get the benefit immediately and can go further. Unfortunately, we have to pay it back and usually with a substantial interest rate. It's better we live a life of steady progress and organic growth.

Practical Ideas On How To Live This Out

I've got boundaries for work. These boundaries include working weekdays only and within forty-five hours. With a wife, four children, and a community I care about, I'm interested in more than just working.

Look at the context of your life including your priorities. Make the decision on how much time you want to budget for each. If you are going to work extra, be intentional with communicating this overage.

A Yearly Blogging Break

I blog regularly. Depending on my workload, the frequency will fluctuate, but I currently update it monthly. At the end of each year, starting with 2014, I've taken a break from blogging for a least a month sometimes two to three.

While blogging is a great outlet with numerous benefits, It can also feel like a burden I've got to keep up. Taking a break provides me the freedom of not updating it. It leads to rejuvenation and new ideas for when I do start back up.

Monthly Days Off

Another rest approach I find value in is taking a day off at the end of a month. It's a day where I take a break from routine responsibilities of life including work and family. The first time I decided to do this, I aligned it with the release date for Fallout 4 where I spent most of the day playing the game on my PC and going out to eat at places I loved. It was a day of enjoyment.

It was a great idea because it led me to work harder and prepare for it, knowing the day off would soon happen. Also, I was rejuvenated by doing something fun and different than my normal life cycles, preparing me for a more productive return to work.

After testing it out, I ended up doing it a few more times where I included my wife. In addition to taking my day off, I also gave her a day off where I watched the kids, and she rested. It was a great experience because it helped remind me of the difficulty she faces in raising our children and gave her a break from the responsibilities of raising our kids.

While this rest cycle is something I want hardwired into our life cycle, having a fourth child placed our rhythms into chaos in 2016. As we got back into a steady schedule a year later, we continued taking these monthly breaks to help us both sustain a healthy life.

Ramping Up & Down

Another helpful rhythm of rest was establishing a daily, weekly, monthly and yearly ramp up and ramp down. For the dailies, there is a series of actions I take in the morning to start my work day. It begins with prayer and focus time and leads to working on paying projects. Ramping down is the time I take to close out my work day and begin thinking about dinner and time with my family.

Here are some examples to inspire.

Daily Ramp Up

- Write what I'm grateful for.
- Review/plan client work for the day.
- Respond to incoming email, text messages and voicemails.

Weekly Ramp Up

- Pray about the upcoming week.
- Check in with clients & communicate the week's goals.
- Follow-up with incoming leads.

Yearly Ramp Down

- Blog post reflecting on the year.
- Cleanup client folders & files.
- Send out thank you messages to clients.

Monthly Ramp Down

- End of month report & message to my wife.
- Reconcile bank account statements.

These on and off ramps help to ease in and out of work and make the transition easier and more pleasurable. They also assist in ensuring I take care of the most important but least urgent tasks. As you establish these habits, keep in mind, they will likely be missed at times because of the circumstances of life. Having them in place helps us reset when we feel like we've lost control.

Checkpoint 4 - Live A Healthier Life

In 2013, life's circumstances pushed in on me and ever since I've been compelled to live a healthier life.

I admit, I'm no health authority. In fact, my favorite Mexican dish is Alambre', which is a fajita type meal where the steak is cooked with bacon and covered in Monterey Jack. While I've got a way to go before I'd stamp myself as an overall healthy eater, I care enough to takes steps towards a healthier life. That's the first key. Are we moving in the right direction?

Early in my transition towards a healthier life, I was doing physical and mental exercises. With the chaos of a changing life, many of these healthier activities got lost as we moved from our home of nine years, north of Atlanta, to a new place several miles east. These changes also coincided with me starting my freelance career and having our third child.

Two years into freelancing, I decided to once again take small steps towards living healthier. One easy way I did this was to shift my daily drinking habits. I enjoy drinking tea, but I was mostly drinking caffeinated black tea with sugar. Daily, I was drinking four cups on average. I decided to replace two of the cups with a green and white tea, and the third cup with a calming or herbal tea. This new approach would cut back on the caffeine and sugar while also providing the health benefits these other teas offered. It was an easy first step that didn't require me to change my deep-rooted habits.

Another example includes my work chair and desktop setup. For most of the day while I'm working, I'm sitting. As a way to work on my core strength and balance, I shifted to sitting on an exercise ball.

While I've worked at one of my client's offices, I've tested working at a standing desk. Again, these are small changes I'm exploring and doing for health benefits.

In the spring of 2016, I decided to start back up with running one and a half miles to and from our local park a dozen times per month. Also, I'd walk the kids to the park several times per week, and work on the yard during weekends. Unfortunately, after several months of doing it consistently, I got sick, and I let the morning activity go.

While It's never easy, the fact that it was now winter made it harder to get out there and do it. In the start of 2017, I bit the bullet and restarted my running habit.

All of these smalls steps to build out new habits lead to a healthier physical life. Let's shift gears and talk about a healthy mental and spiritual life.

Journaling, Prayer, & Brain Exercises

I began journaling in 2010 using the highly helpful and useful Evernote software. With over thirteen hundred notes, I've put it to great use.

Journaling helps us to articulate what is going on in our life. Through the process of writing, we learn to articulate how we feel, and it becomes an outlet to process our emotions. What we can learn from the situations we encounter along our life's journey is powerful and something journaling facilitates. It gives us a point of reference to see how far we've matured as time passes by. It provides us with an outlet to share our thoughts and ideas with others. Journaling helps us keep our mind active and to sharpen and empty it so we can move forward wherever we feel stuck.

Another way to keep our mind active is by engaging in puzzles and mind games. For years, I enjoyed working the New York Times crossword puzzles that came to me through one of my early jobs. In the past few years, I've found the brain games from Lumosity to be a great way to keep my mind sharp and focused. In addition to strengthening our brain, it's also quite fun.

Another outlet for growing is by listening to podcasts. For me, I tend to be on the road quite a bit each week. These extended periods of driving are great times for listening to podcasts about God, life, politics, culture, and other topics of interest. Always be learning is a value of high worth to me and listening to insights helps me grow.

While keeping our mind and heart fine-tuned are essential to succeeding at the highest level of freelancing, we also need not neglect our spirit.

Since I was young, I've engaged in a regular prayer life sharing my gratitude and needs with the creator of the universe. I think of prayer as a conversation between a friend and me, but instead of a friend, it's my heavenly father who knit every part of me while I incubated in my mom's womb (*Psalms 139:13-14*). There have been times where I've neglected this and times of suffering where I've cried out in desperation. What I know from prayer is that it changes and aligns me with God and his essential nature of love, relationship, community and justice. If you lack a belief in a personal creator of the universe, take the time to be still, clear your mind and reflect.

Deciding to live a healthier physical, mental and spiritual life, can start by simply identifying small steps and moving forward with them. It does not have to be complicated or sophisticated, just start doing it.

Is Freelancing The Launching Pad Or The Destination?

Unifying freelancing means we understand that our destination affects us both personally and professionally. For some of us, we desire to freelance as a long term career commitment, while others see it as an opportunity to bridge a gap as we make progress towards a goal outside freelancing.

For me, I fall into the latter. While I enjoy freelancing and am skilled at it, it is a three to five year season of my life where it will become less prominent as I generate an income from writing. My plan beyond freelancing as a marketer is to dive deeper into storytelling through writing with the intent to get involved in the film industry as a screenwriter and director. While I'll still be a "freelancer", my craft and customers will shift dramatically.

I could make the decision to stop freelancing as a communication specialist and jump full-time into writing, selling books and doing speaking events, but this can be a tough venture. By having a wife and four kids, there are realities and responsibilities I face which make it risky and difficult to make a dramatic leap. I've also done this type of jump in the past, and I'm no longer energized and equipped to make that sort of drastic change in this season of life.

There is a friend of mine who was making good money at his job. While employed, he authored a compelling book about entrepreneurship. After he had finished writing the book, he decided to quit his job and become a full-time speaker and author.

What he soon realized is how difficult it was to make his dream a sustainable one for him and his family. His funds ran out, and he ended up pausing his dream to get a new job where he could provide for his family. There will be a time in his future where he'll be able to move further down the road he started, but he injected a large delay in getting to his destination.

The alternative to the dramatic leap is to build the foundation of the new direction and make the slow progression as the platform is strengthened over time. When we identify the thousand baby steps to get there, we can take them before we're forced to fully transition. There will always be some risk and faith required, but we can wisely proceed to maximize our chances of success and minimize the consequences of the risk that may ensue.

For those who are single, have more flexibility and margin, consider doing the most dramatic. Live simply and take a leap towards your dreams. It may be the last time you get the opportunity to do it.

Wrapping Up The Seventh Achievement

As freelancers, we want unity with our clients, but it's the unity we have in our personal lives that sustains us over the long and difficult journey. When we harness the expected and unexpected circumstances to align our personal and professional lives, we excel in meaningful ways. We also do our loved ones well by bringing them along and allowing participation in the journey.

Let's review the four checkpoints we'll pass as we bring our personal and work lives into alignment.

1. Responsive Personal Budget
2. We Bring Our Family (or Close Friends) Along
3. Active Rhythms Of Rest & Release
4. Live A Healthier Life

To complete this achievement, we don't just balance personal and work, we unify both to work on the other's behalf. This is thriving together, and while this may feel like the last achievement, there's one more.

When I first compiled these seven achievements, it covered everything I'd journeyed through. But, I realized there was a missing piece I had yet to walk forward on. Legacy. What was I going to do to pass on what I knew to others that would follow after me?

The desire to share what I mastered grew as I realized freelancing was a transitionary stage towards my goal of film direction. If I passed through freelancing and moved on, I've helped myself progress, but I've also hoarded the insights that could help other freelancers prosper. It turns out when we take the time to teach and share with others, both the teacher and the student benefit.

Vital Achievement #8
We Share What We've Mastered

What if every leader and artist in history chose not to share their wisdom with the generation to follow? It'd stagnate innovation, delay progress and make it difficult for the next generation. Not sharing is what it means to hoard what we've mastered, the opposite aim of this achievement.

After moving to Atlanta, I became a student of several toxic mentors. Life and work got harder over the following years. It wasn't until a supportive friend and leader took me under his wing in an ongoing and long-term basis to share what he knew and listen to my struggles. His demonstrated leadership and inspired me to do the same for others.

Teaching what we know provides us the opportunity to translate what we know in our head into words and practices others can replicate in their lives. It allows us to understand our success better as well as identify gaps in our knowledge and understanding.

So, it turns out if we choose not to share what we've mastered with others, we not only neglect the next generation; we lose out on the many gems and benefits this process surfaces.

How do we know we're moving towards completing this achievement? Let's jump into the first checkpoint and find out.

CheckPoint 1 - Sharing Insights With Others

Several months into my freelancing journey, a new friend from Twitter informed me he was going to leave his corporate job and work full time as a freelancer.

Each and every challenge he was likely going to encounter for the next twelve months flashed through my mind. I was compelled to warn him of what was to come so he could make wise decisions and prepare accordingly.

We had numerous conversations discussing freelancing and systems I developed to help me succeed. We also discussed my failures and how I overcame them. In fact, many of these discussions led to the content in this book.

I want others to learn from my mistakes, so they don't have to struggle like I did. If they do make the same error, I want to provide a great resource to help them climb out of their problems.

In addition to sharing insights with my Twitter friend, I had a client who bought me a series of lunches so he could ask me questions about the type of work I do, and how I managed projects so efficiently.

These two instances turned into a pattern where clients and friends were connecting me with others who needed the insights I was willing to share. The value provided was so strong certain clients were paying me to share them with their team.

Feeling The Pain Points

In the last decade of my life, I've gone through an unusually large amount of positive and negatives experiences. I got married, moved across the country, went to college, started a political news website, attempted to make a feature film and launched a marketing agency. As a result, I've accumulated wounds and scars tied to these experiences. While these wounds were difficult to heal from, it's the point when I could help others from those places of pain that I had a positive and significant impact on the lives of others. In fact, many of my pain points act as triggers for me to engage in the life of other people.

One freelancing friend was struggling in the context of his spiritual journey and romantic relationships. After I met him, I immediately reached out to listen and share insights. It was his struggles I could relate to because I had gone through similar ones myself.

On another note, I became friends with a fellow contractor working for a mutual client. Unfortunately, the client's business went under in a tragic way. Both I and my new friend lost two thousand unpaid dollars. From our newly formed bond and out of this shared negative experience, it helped us connect and continue to walk alongside each other in our respective freelancing journeys.

The third example of me seeing someone experience a pain point was the spouse of a high school church friend who recently moved to Atlanta with his family. I immediately thought of the tough transition I went through moving across the country from Arizona to Atlanta Georgia. Because of the connection and the personal pain point reminder, I wanted to do what I could to help.

Helping others driven by the wounds we've had, can be a deeply healing process and one that comes with meaning.

The reception of my help from others is validation of my insights and ideas. This led me to realize it was time to share these insights beyond one-on-one encounters.

 WE'RE BROADCASTING OUR INSIGHTS

 We **write** and **share** our insights in simple and public form for the benefit of others.

Share on **social media, blogs** and **private messages**.

Checkpoint 2 - Broadcasting Our Insights

As individuals, we're limited in time for sharing with others. A powerful way to increase our capacity and help more people is to write and share through private messages or in a public forum like social media or a blog.

I had a friend whose income stream dried up and he needed to generate revenue quickly. As we spoke, I listed several activities he could do today to get traction and move to where he needed to be. It resulted in the blog post, "10 Simple Actions Freelancers Need To Do When Income Dries Up", which you read earlier in this book.

Within the next month, there were two more people with whom I shared the article. Once it was written, I had completed the hard work. For every additional person that needs it, I simply share the link.

It was this same type of experience I discovered after I started privately journaling in 2010. When others in my life experienced similar struggles, I shared my personal journal pages as a way to teach and inspire them. Several years later, I made the decision to blog publicly on a regular basis shortly before I began freelancing in early 2014. With this available resource, I've personally shared different written posts with others who could specifically benefit from the content.

Capture Our Conversations

So, here is a key in easily creating content we can share. When we discuss ideas with others, we tend to have insights and epiphanies. The next time this happens, simply capture the insight and spend five to ten minutes writing it into a short, simple blog post. The difficulty of writing is usually thinking and challenging the insight. Since we're doing this in our conversation naturally, the hard part is done. Let's harvest our fruit by writing and sharing it instead of allowing it to fade away.

Writing helps us to organize and clarify our ideas. It gives others the opportunity to act on these ideas to make their situation better. Writing is a powerful outlet. It builds our business and helps others grow theirs. When we're actively publishing our insights, we know we're moving closer to mastery of our work.

Regularly writing and sharing life with others has its limits. Once we face that realization, we'll become motivated to help others apply the words into their lives through ongoing hands-on relationships.

Checkpoint 3 - Actively Mentoring

With enough people seeking us out to share insights on the work we do and how we do it, it's a good time to dive into the lives of others and facilitate individual and group mentoring.

Three people were asking to meet up and discuss the freelance systems and insights I leveraged. Eventually, the requests mounted up, and I launched a freelancing group where we could discuss the eight vital achievements on a monthly basis. This meeting would help them grow as freelancers while allowing me to receive feedback and accountability to finish the book. It was the monthly group that pushed me to get each achievement's graphics for this book completed.

As the group progressed, some people fell off, and others were invited to join in their places. It turned out to be a fruitful exercise for those involved, helping them at different points in their journey.

Be The Vision

When we mentor others, we soon discover how it elevates us to the highest level of freelancing. As a leader, we want to be an example of the vision we're casting and the model of what we believe they too can become. Living as a public example of the progress and regress we experience is inspiring and empowering. It provides us motivation to continue forward when we've lost the energy to do so.

As we share with others, they provide feedback, pushback, and challenges to what we bring to the table. These act as powerful opportunities to refine our work into something more compelling and effective. It is the monthly meetings that elevated Path Of The Freelancer to the rich content you now read. Others help us keep our ego in check and see our blind spots.

Once we've seen the positive impact we have on the lives of others, we're compelled to take the final step in leaving a legacy to those that will come after us. It is by implementing a program for teaching beyond ourselves that we accomplish this desire.

4 PERMANENT BEYOND-US SYSTEM

We've Created A Way For The World To
Learn, **Share** and **Teach** What We've Mastered.

Checkpoint 4 - Permanent Beyond-Us System

For some, freelancing is the destination, and for others, including myself, freelancing is a transitional season. In either case, there will be a time when we no longer freelance.

My personal goal is to create a financially sustainable writing career, and I chose the topic of freelancing because I could have the highest impact for myself and others. Borrowing from my business ownership days and thinking through how to apply those concepts in freelancing provided the greatest impact least resistant path to publishing a book. I simply had to take what was in my head and behavior and transcribe it for the benefit of others. It was the best natural next step on my trajectory.

The value I bring to freelancers is the insights and experience from owning and running a business. To Infuse these in freelancing is to create something new, compelling and effective for those who do not think in the way I have.

With a finite timeline, finishing well as a freelancer meant capturing and publishing my insights for the long term benefit of others. Writing a book and supplementing it with relevant and effective resources is what I leave to you and others.

This final step in mastering our craft is teaching the teachers. Teaching students is one of the last steps, but it's not until we teach teachers that we're able to see everything come full circle and make sense of how it all comes together.

I've written this book and provided a comprehensive website to teach students who want to learn, and to equip teachers to carry these concepts to the next generations of Freelancers.

With them in place, I no longer am necessary for the flourishing of other freelancers, and I've finished my mission in creating a permanent beyond-me system.

Wrapping Up The Eighth Achievement

While it may not seem intuitive, it is not until we actively share what we've mastered that we arrive at a complete state of flourishing as a freelancer.

Some benefits we receive are immediate and others are long-term. Some are superficial and others deeply meaningful. Sometimes we help others more than they help us and vice versa.

When we've done this achievement well, we've played a role guiding people into a state of flourishing, and we've left behind valuable insights and resources that guide others beyond our death or departure.

The following four checkpoints we've walked through help us sustain the eighth and final achievement.

1. We're Sharing Insights With Others
2. We're Broadcasting Our Insights
3. We're Actively Mentoring
4. Permanent Beyond-Us System

Which checkpoints have you explored? Which have you passed? Which are you currently sustaining?

Like the last step in alcoholics anonymous, it's not until we embrace this last achievement of helping others that we'll fully master the business and craft of freelancing. If you've hit a wall or are struggling, the key may be to teach and inspire others who are earlier in their journey. While it may feel like doing so will take away from your effort to succeed, the reality is quite the opposite. Make the time to help someone else. Share what you've mastered.

Our Personal Achievement Strategy

We've explored all eight achievements. Now, you may wonder where you go from here. Ultimately, we want to sustain all checkpoints for all of the achievements. So, our first step is to look in the mirror and evaluate where we stand in each area. Self-evaluation is how we discover this.

Before we get started, let's revisit the eight vital achievements.

1. Fully Committed To Freelance
2. Offerings In A Compelling Package
3. Steady Stream Of Paying Clients
4. Active Clients Are Maximized
5. Unaffected By The Roller Coaster
6. Wise & Precise Financial Management
7. Unified Personal & Work Lives
8. We Share What We've Mastered

Self-Evaluation

As part of the evaluation, we'll use the stages of commitment to guide us in determining where we are in each checkpoint within each achievement. The following sections will guide in better understanding where you are so you can better map out your progress to the destination. It also acts as a powerful review of all the achievements and checkpoints we've discussed in the book. Let's get at it!

Achievement #1: Fully Committed To Freelance

As you reflect on the eight achievements and the overall vocation of freelancing, circle the level of commitment that most accurately reflects where you are right now?

Survivor	Dreamer	Visionary	Achiever
Open	Discovering	Starting	Sustaining
Closed	Avoiding	Abandoned	Concluded

Are you a survivor focused on getting through the day with little regard to what's ahead or behind? Are you closed to ideas or open to the potential of freelancing?

Are you a dreaming freelancer? Are you discovering the concept, excited about what could be ahead in your journey? Have you completed your discovery and are now avoiding taking the first step towards your goal?

Are you a visionary freelancer who's started freelancing but still trying to figure out what path to take? Have you found yourself starting many pathways without following through on any of them? When things get tough, do you find yourself seeking traditional employment instead of your next gig?

Are you an achieving freelancer who sustains a strong vocation? When you face obstacles do you simply figure out how to overcome them instead of turning back? Or have you explored, tested and found freelancing is not the path you'd like to take, and you've intentionally chosen to close the door?

Take a moment and decide what your level of commitment is as a freelancer. When would you like to progress to the next stage? *Write your answer below.*

As we explore the other seven achievements, we'll evaluate them within this lens. Our goal is to identify where we are for each checkpoint. There is a chart at the end of each achievement for you to write your stage for each one.

Achievement #2: Offerings In A Compelling Package

When we package our offerings in a compelling way, we've set the stage for an easier journey in freelancing. Knowing what we offer, how we work with others and articulating this in writing, gives us an upper hand in achieving our goals. Publishing our information is when we put the package to the test.

As you evaluate the four checkpoints listed for this section, reflect on each and think about where you think you are at in the spectrum (Survivor, Dreamer, Visionary, Achiever).

Remember, there is no right answer. This assessment is designed to help you better understand your progress and where your strengths and weaknesses lie. To help guide you, I've provided some directional examples for each checkpoint.

Compensation Is Set

If you're wondering what compensation means as a freelancer, you're likely a survivor for this checkpoint. If you're exploring the methods of compensation and which is right for you, you're likely a dreamer. If you've tried out different compensation approaches but have yet to commit to one, you're likely a visionary. If you've determined and maintained your compensation goals, you're an achiever.

How & What We Offer Is Defined

If you don't know the services you'll offer and the process to follow when working with clients, you're probably a survivor. If you've explored different activities to serve customers but have yet to do any of them, you're most likely a dreamer. If you're experimenting with your offerings but have yet to nail it down, you're usually a visionary. If you know how you serve clients and can easily articulate it, you're an achiever for this checkpoint.

Our Package Is Published

If you don't know what your freelancing solution package is, you're a survivor. If you've planned the publishing of your offerings but have yet to execute that plan, you're no doubt a dreamer. If you've published your package but aren't completely confident with what you've put out there, you're likely a visionary for the checkpoint. If you've skillfully crafted and published what you do and how you work with customers, you're an achiever.

Our Personal Brand Is Promoted

If you're not sure you'll promote yourself as an individual or a company, you're probably a survivor. If you're exploring your personal brand and how it could help you to get out there, you're possibly a dreamer. If you've put yourself out there publicly as a way to grow your freelancing business, you're perhaps a visionary. If you're sustaining a public brand consistently, you're an achiever.

Grade Yourself

Using the right column on the following chart, indicate next to each checkpoint where you believe you currently stand.

Checkpoints	Your Current Stage
1. Compensation Is Set	
2. How & What We Offer Is Defined	
3. Our Package Is Published	
4. Our Personal Brand Is Promoted	

Achievement #3: Steady Stream Of Paying Clients

When we've succeeded at this achievement, we've successfully found clients, established a sales process, built a team of advocates and established authority for attracting potential customers. Use the following examples and direction to help you discover which stage you fall under.

We're Finding New Projects

If you've got no idea you need to find new projects to succeed as a freelancer, you're a survivor. If you've thought about where you could meet potential new customers, you're a dreamer. If you've sold your first deal but haven't made much progress beyond that, you're presumably a visionary. If you can consistently recruit new clients, you're an achiever.

Sales Is A Predictable Process

If you go about sales without thinking about it, you're likely a survivor. If you've thought about how you can be more thoughtful with your sales efforts, you're probably a dreamer for this checkpoint. If you've set up a sales process but have since abandoned it because you didn't like it or were not willing to follow it, you're a visionary. If you've set and consistently followed a sales process, you're an achiever.

We've Built A Team Of Advocates

If you're operating on your own, you're a survivor for this checkpoint. If you've thought about your team of advocates but have not talked to them, you're likely a dreamer. If you've spoken to some advocates and received a deal or two from them, you're perhaps a visionary. If you've got a great group of people who send work your way, you're an achiever.

Referrals & Leads Seek Us Out

Not sure what a referral is? You're a survivor. Think it'd be great to have referrals and leads seeking us out? You're probably a dreamer. If you've had a referral or two reach out to you, you're likely a visionary for this checkpoint. If you've got a steady amount of leads contacting you, you're an achiever.

Assess Where You Are

Take a moment and write below the stage you see yourself in for the following four checkpoints.

Checkpoints	Your Current Stage
1. We're Finding New Projects	
2. Sales Is A Predictable Process	
3. We've Built A Team Of Advocates	
4. Referrals & Leads Seek Us Out	

Achievement #4: We're Maximizing Our Active Clients

Success in this achievement means we've tapped into our lowest hanging fruit. Existing clients hold the easiest path for increasing our income, but it requires relational prioritization. Once we've learned to expand our services and generate passive income streams, we'll move towards a state where we work in ongoing engagements with only our sweet spot clients.

Cultivate Client Relationships

If you work with your clients but don't to anything beyond that, you're likely a survivor. If you wish you could build relationships with your clients, but don't try, you're probably a dreamer. If you've built relational equity with some customers, you're presumably a visionary. If you actively build relationships with all of your clients, you're an achiever for this checkpoint.

Passive Income Streams

If you've never even thought of passive income streams as a freelancer, you're a survivor. If you've researched and found different options, but have yet to sell any, you're a dreamer for this checkpoint. If you've got a few clients paying for your passive income services, you're probably a visionary. If you consistently share and sell your passive income services to all your clients, you're an achiever.

Ongoing Client Engagements

If you only focus on finishing a project and moving on to each client, you're presumably a survivor. If you've thought and speculated about working with clients beyond the project, you're most likely a dreamer. If you've transformed, by accident, a project into an ongoing engagement, you're likely a visionary. If you consistently morph project clients into perpetual projects, you're an achiever.

Sweet Spot Clients Only

If you don't know what a sweet spot client looks like for you, you're a survivor. If you've imagined what it would be like to have a sweet spot client, but have never experienced one, you're a dreamer. If you've worked with a sweet spot client on occasion, you're probably a visionary. If most or all of your customers are sweet spot clients, you're an achiever.

Self Assessment

Before you proceed to the next achievement, reflect on the following four checkpoints and determine which stage you believe you're in.

Checkpoints	Current Stage
1. Cultivate Client Relationships	
2. Passive Income Streams	
3. Ongoing Client Engagements	
4. Sweet Spot Clients Only	

Achievement #5: Unaffected By The Roller Coaster

In the classic Greek story of Sisyphus, he's forced to push a boulder up a mountain only for it to roll back down to push again. As a freelancer, the roller coaster of going up and down can easily feel like Sisyphus' eternal consequence. Thankfully, with some focus and discipline, we can establish powerful structures to allow us to make progress and move beyond the roller coaster. Use the following direction to help you understand what stage you find yourself in for each checkpoint.

Color Zone System Is Active

If you've never thought about how you'll respond to the ups and downs of freelancing, you're possibly a survivor. If you've wished you had a way to deal with the roller coaster effect, you're probably a dreamer. If you've started building and doing a set of activities to help you during the slow times, you're likely a visionary. If you've got a plan in place that you easily execute when things are rough, you're an achiever.

Emotional Support System

If you're all alone in freelancing, you're a survivor for this checkpoint. If you hope to have people from whom you could receive encouragement and support, you're probably a dreamer. If you've got a supportive friend or two, by accident, you're possibly a visionary. If you've intentionally crafted a close and extended community to help you with the ups and downs of freelancing, you're an achiever.

The Water Tower

You're a survivor for this checkpoint if you've never thought of a fund to help alleviate the financial droughts. You're prone to dreaming if you've imagined not struggling when work was slow. You're likely a visionary if you've set aside some funds for a rainy day. If you've established a water tower number and grown your cash flow to that number, you've achieved for this checkpoint.

Water Tower Management System

If you've not thought beyond today or this week financially, you're probably a survivor. You're plausibly a dreamer if you've only learned about how you can save for the future. Seemingly, you're a visionary if you've begun saving for your future. If you've set up a plan for the short, medium and long term and are well on your way to completing it, you're an achiever.

Self Evaluation

With the provided examples, take a moment to fill out the chart for the following four checkpoints. Write down where you see yourself in each stage.

Checkpoints	Current Stage
1. Color Zone System (CZS) Is Active	
2. Emotional Support System	
3. The Water Tower	
4. Water Tower Management System	

Achievement #6: Wise & Precise Financial Management

While possibly the least exciting of the achievements, wise and precise financial management may be the most important to sustain. When we see and respond accurately to our context and towards our goals, we're able to make real and meaningful progress. For the following four checkpoints, think about how you fare for this achievement.

Legit Business & Bank Account

If you operate as yourself using personal bank accounts, you're a survivor. If you've thought you need to do things differently by separating your personal and business dealings, you're a dreamer. As a visionary, you've most likely started the process of launching a business and beginning a bank account. As an achiever, you've established them and actively use them to your advantage.

We're Easily Watching What We Track

If you don't know how much money you have or make and don't know how to spend your time, you're a survivor. If you're discovering how to track your time and money, you've moved from a survivor to a dreamer. If you've set up some tools to track your money and time, but don't follow through consistently your possibly a visionary. If you've allocated every dollar and minute of your time to a particular purpose, you're an achiever for this checkpoint.

We're Paid On-Time

If you don't even know what invoices are due and what is late, you're likely a survivor. If you've dreamed of clients paying you on time or early but think of it as impossible, you're probably a dreamer. As a visionary, you receive payment early sometimes, but not usually. As an achiever, you're almost always paid on-time or early.

Payroll & Taxes Are Turnkey

If you have not yet filed taxes since you began freelancing, you're a survivor. If you've explored some options for making taxes easier and streamlined, you're possibly a dreamer. If you've started using some services or tools to help manage taxes and payroll, you're a visionary. If you've got a reliable system you follow with strict adherence; you're an achiever.

Self Reflection

Take a moment below and write in what you think you are for each checkpoint.

Checkpoints	Current Stage
1. Legit Business & Bank Accounts	
2. We're Easily Watching What We Track	
3. We're Paid On-Time	
4. Payroll & Taxes Are Turnkey	

Achievement #7: Unified Personal & Work Lives

Operating our personal and professional lives in sync is a beautiful way to abide. It requires intentionality and hard work, but the fruit of our labor is well worth the effort. Are you in sync already or are you in the midst of fragmentation? Take a look below to explore where you might align with the checkpoints from this achievement.

Responsive Personal Budget

If you spend as money comes in, you're quite possibly a survivor. If you're a dreamer, you've recognized a lack of unity between your spending and income and seek resolution. If you've started a budget to help bring the two in alignment, you're a visionary. If you consistently maintain and follow a responsive budget, you're an achiever.

We Bring Our Family (Or Close Friends) Along

If we don't even know who is affected by our freelancing, we're a survivor. For dreamers, they've likely realized how their freelancing work affects other people. Visionaries have started communicating with their spouse, kids or close friends about their journey. Achievers have open and consistent communication with those closest to them and affected by their work.

Active Rhythms Of Rest & Release

If you don't rest, you're a survivor. If you've thought about ways and times you could spend relaxing; you're likely a dreamer. If you've tried different approaches to taking time off and relaxing from work, but have not maintained these over time, you're probably a visionary. If you have active rhythms of rest, release and ramping up and down, you're an achiever.

Live A Healthier Life

Don't physically feel good but don't care why? You're likely a survivor. Do you think about and explore ways you can eat and exercise but don't yet act on it? You're a dreamer. Have you tried a diet or started an exercise program but have left it in the dust? If so, you're a visionary. If eating well and physical activity is part of your routine, you're an achiever.

Stage Identification

Using the chart below, scribble down what step you believe you're in for each checkpoint.

Checkpoints	Current Stage
1. Responsive Personal Budget	
2. We Bring Our Family (Or Close Friends) Along	
3. Active Rhythms Of Rest & Release	
4. Live A Healthier Life	

Achievement #8: We Share What We Mastered

The final achievement is not about us. It's about bringing other potential and actual freelancers to a state of mastery. It is this achievement where we teach freelancers and extend our legacy of skills and experiences to those who follow in our footsteps. While it can be difficult, it is also highly meaningful. Use the following guide to determine what accomplishments you've made in this arena.

Sharing Insights With Others

If you keep your ideas, stories, and insights to yourself, you're plausibly a survivor. If you've thought about sharing with others but decided not to, you're a dreamer. If you've shared some insights when others requested it, you're probably a visionary. If you consistently share your insights with others who ask or those you think would benefit, you're an achiever.

Broadcasting Insights

If you're not open to the idea of publishing your thoughts and insights publicly, you're a survivor. If you've imagined what it'd be like for others to ask for your advice, you're probably a dreamer. If you've posted a few articles randomly on social media, you're likely a visionary. If you actively write and share your wisdom, you're an achiever.

Actively Mentoring

If you've not focused on anyone outside of yourself, you're likely a survivor. If you've been thinking about helping another freelancer master their craft, you're possibly a dreamer. If you've mentored a person or two along your journey, you're a visionary for this checkpoint. If you actively find and mentor others, you're an achiever.

Permanent Beyond-Us System

If you don't even know what a beyond-us system is, you're most likely a survivor. If you think about legacy and what you might leave behind when you die, you might be a dreamer. If you've started to create something that could last beyond you, you're a visionary for this checkpoint. If you're actively creating and sharing in permanent formats, you're an achiever.

Final Self Appraisal

For the last achievement, take a second and write down which stage you fall into for each checkpoint.

Checkpoints	Current Stage
1. Sharing Insights With Others	
2. Broadcasting Insights	
3. Actively Mentoring	
4. Permanent Beyond-Us System	

Let's Prioritize

Whew! While that may have felt a bit repetitive, it was an important activity to help assess where we are and also to engrain the achievements and checkpoints further into our minds.

Now that we know where we stand, it's up to you to take steps towards improving. Review the achievements in the following chart and number them in order of priority from one to eight, with one indicating most important.

Fully Committed To Freelance	
Offerings In A Compelling Package	
Steady Stream Of Paying Clients	
Active Clients Are Maximized	
Unaffected By The Roller Coaster	
Wise & Precise Financial Management	
Unified Personal & Work Lives	
We Share What We've Mastered	

You've now set the stage for how you'll prioritize improving your freelance business. What was most important in the list? Why did you place it at the top? What was least important? Why? *(Write it below)*

Excellent work. You've now mapped the high-level pathway you'll take towards flourishing in freelancing. Your next step is to get specific.

Take a moment and review how you graded yourself from the checkpoints review exercise. In the chart below, indicate the top three most important checkpoints you need to work on over the next three months.

Great work. Think about why you chose these three checkpoints as most important. Imagine what it will be like when you've mastered all three.

Alright, let's break it down into actionable items. Over the next thirty days, what three actions will you take to move forward on these three checkpoints? When will you complete each action? *Use the column on the right to input your due date.*

Congratulations. You've now learned of all eight achievements and established an action plan to move forward.

If you're starting freelancing fresh and you work on one checkpoint every twenty days, you'll be fully up and running within eighteen months of your starting date. If you've already been freelancing for some time, you'll be able to get up and running much quicker.

Flourishing as a freelancer is within your grasps.

Will you act on it?

You Are The Freelancer, Help Pave The Path For Those To Follow

As you pass a majority of these checkpoints, your final step is to help bring other freelancers along. It is you and others who will bring these eight achievements to life.

Learn from them.

Master and modify them.

Make them better and pass them along.

What are you waiting for?

Get started!

Acknowledgements

I could not have completed my first book without the help and support of those I love and who love me.

We thrive together.

Thank you, Jesus, for the love, grace and opportunity provided for me to write Path Of The Freelancer. The abundance of provision, support, insights and community was invaluable and deeply appreciated in completing this task.

Thank you to my lovely and enduring wife, and all four loving and giving children, Madison, David, Judah, and Elihu. I appreciate your sacrifice in time and focus as I spent the time to write this book.

Thank you, Jim Karwisch, for your friendship, time discussing the concepts in this book and for sharing life with me.

Thank you, Keith Taylor, for writing the introduction, sharing your feedback and faithfulness in helping me make Path Of The Freelancer better.

Thank you Addison Williams for living out the concepts in this book. You were a real-time living case study!

Thank you, Toby Bloomberg, Fred Hadra, Dean Carrera, Craig Williams, Allison Miller, Fred Spring, and Syd Walker for your friendship, participation, and collaboration to make Path Of The Freelancer better.

Thank you, Len Wikberg and Beth Coetzee, for your friendship, insights, and support during the years of Noodlehead Marketing. Much of what is in this book is an evolution of what we learned together. Thank you, Len, for helping me to make the book cover better.

Thank you to all who shared a small insight or feedback for making the book better.

Additional Resources

The Path Of The Freelancer website is full of resources including an online toolbox, achievement library, and directory of freelancers.

Find and explore at www.pathofthefreelancer.com

If you'd like to take a deeper dive, please share a copy of the book with a friend and meet regularly to discuss.

If you'd like to lead a mastermind group of freelancers, we've set up an online resource center to help you facilitate the meetings.

About The Author

Working with his uncle's animation studio, in high school and shortly after, Jason Scott Montoya worked on projects for PBS, Discovery Channel and several museums around the world.

The day after he and his wife returned from their honeymoon in 2005, they packed up everything and moved on a leap of faith from Arizona to Atlanta. He graduated in 2008 from the Art Institute of Atlanta with a bachelor's degree in media and animation, attempted to make a feature film, launched a political news website, ran a marketing agency, and had four kids in twelve years.

He's a follower of the Way, the Truth and the Life, a husband, father, teacher and storyteller. He believes in sharing good, and not so good, stories from his journey as a way to process ideas and inspire others.

In his journey, he's experienced and seen others experience the life of surviving in isolation. In these times of need, others helped and encouraged him when he needed it.

As a result, his personal aim is to inspire others to a place of thriving and togetherness, which means living in healthy community with others. One where his relationship with God, family, community and country are lived out as a positive example. An example others would aspire.

Learn more about Jason on his website at www.jasonscottmontoya.com.

Speaking On Freelancing

Are you interested in hiring Jason Montoya to speak about Freelancing at your event?

He speaks at a high level about the eight achievements from the book or he can take a deeper dive on one of the specific eight achievements teaching the contained checkpoints.

For those interested, please visit www.PathOfTheFreelancer.com/speaking for more information.

64099293R00153

Made in the USA
Lexington, KY
28 May 2017